BONDING
WITH
GOD

A Reflective Study of
Biblical Covenant

ROLAND J. FALEY, T.O.R.

PAULIST PRESS
New York ◆ Mahwah, N.J.

All scripture quotations are from the *New American Bible*.

Cover design by Cindy Dunne.

Library of Congress Cataloging-in-Publication Data

Faley, Roland J. (Roland James), 1930–
    Bonding with God : a reflective study of biblical covenant / Roland J. Faley.
      p. cm.
    Includes bibliographical references and index.
    ISBN 0-8091-3706-2 (alk. paper)
    1. Covenants (Theology)–Biblical teaching. 2. Bible–Study and teaching. I. Title.
BS680.C67F35 1997
231.7′6–dc21   97-5314
                                                 CIP

Published by Paulist Press
997 Macarthur Boulevard
Mahwah, New Jersey 07430

Printed and bound in the
United States of America

CONTENTS

*To My Students
at Home and Abroad
Over a Span of Forty Years*

IN GRATITUDE

INTRODUCTION

This book is both a study and a meditation. In looking at the biblical covenant as central to an authentic appreciation of our religious tradition, it will hopefully serve the interests of both the student and the prayerful reflector. Any understanding of the Christian life must ultimately root itself in the fact that God has espoused a people. Thus, it is my hope that this book, centered on the covenant, will lend itself to a deepening of faith on the part of the reader and will open new doors to the ways in which faith expresses itself. While it may serve a variety of needs, it is primarily geared to the needs of those who find in the scriptures the primary source of their faith experience. Although I attempt to incorporate and evaluate critically the results of modern scholarship, my principal aim is to help those who see their life in God as enriched by a better knowledge of the scriptures. In short, this is a book that springs from faith and moves toward faith.

A second reason that prompted its composition is the oft-repeated request, especially from those involved in religious education, for a comprehensive and thematic approach to the major biblical concepts. Obviously *berith* is high on the list. Topical studies as well as commentaries on individual books are indispensable; also helpful are studies that weave together the thread of central concepts which appear in the books of both Testaments. I first attempted to do this in an earlier work that dealt with the question of sin, suffering, and death. Later, after teaching a course in the biblical theology of covenant, it seemed to me that this topic too merited a study, especially for the needs of the nonspecialist. What one may expect to find here is a treatment of the *berith* as it developed within Israel and Christianity and its meaning for the Christian life today. Belief in the centrality of the theme is not forced when one considers that it is the term *covenant,* or *testament,* that specifies the two eras of our faith tradition.

In light of this purpose I have kept in mind the needs of both the classroom and the parish discussion group. A college course on the church, for example, would hopefully find here a useful text, with the chapters so arranged to encompass a semester's work. Scripture-study groups may well find the book helpful in understanding the biblical foundations of the church. Finally, I hope that individual readers will find the book helpful on their faith journey.

I have attempted to focus on each major turning point in the covenant's long history. The reader, of course, will be the best judge of how effectively this has been accomplished. The book is offered with the hope that covenant's relatedness to important features of our faith life—the divine-human interplay, community, worship, sacrifice, eucharist, and the ongoing role of Christ—will be well served by this initiative.

Most of the ideas in this book were tested on my students over the years. Their contribution to refining my thought played a considerable role in determining the shape the book would take. To the theological students who enrolled in "Covenant Theology" at the Oblate School of Theology in San Antonio, Texas, and at the Seminary of the Immaculate Conception in Huntington, New York, I am especially grateful.

1

The Covenant at Sinai

"In this is love: not that we have loved God, but that he loved us."
(1 Jn 4:10)

Life in our times is marked by a loneliness, an incredible feeling of isolation. We hear much about the "global community" and feel so little a part of it. It is the tragic rather than the inspiring that is so much with us. The meaning of neighborhood is lost when so many people scarcely know the occupants of the adjacent apartments. In a very mobile society, where maintaining a job may mean relocation several times, life does not lend itself to a sense of solidarity. Marriages begun in bliss turn sour and leave people endless nights to mourn their plight. Children left to their own resources at an early age become submerged in a street culture that often leads to frustration, crime, even death. Sex is genital release and passing pleasure, detached from any real sense of personhood and abiding love. And so our isolation and withdrawal are drowned in addictions corresponding to every imaginable appetite.

Faith offers more than a modicum of consolation for those who seek meaning in their lives. But for many its message is anything but clear, with the service of God reduced to a series of "dos" and "don'ts." The Judeo-Christian tradition is not a religion of seeking God, but rather one of having been grasped by God. It is, moreover, a faith that binds us together as a community on terms far stronger than social need. Our whole religious tradition finds its beginnings in tribal unity. Our beginnings are not found in a desire for a personal relationship with the deity but rather with a band of displaced persons, called together by a

God who saw them as his "special possession" (Ex 19:5). It is that story which will be retold here, not to solve all our human problems, but simply to illustrate that our times are much at odds with the ways of God. If we could recapture something of what it means to be God's people, we would be motivated as individuals and as a church to find ways to overcome the weariness and aridity of our age. God has bonded with us, and we with God. In biblical terms that means we have strong ties with one another.

The Term Covenant. There is no idea in the Bible richer and more fundamental than covenant. As Walter Eichrodt argued strongly decades ago, it is the "glue" that holds biblical faith together.[1] It is unfortunate that the word itself has no common coinage today. Continued use has offered a certain measure of resuscitation, yet in some way it lacks the richness the word *berith* and its attendant biblical metaphors express. The later *testament* in Greek and Latin translated the original *berith* and, in fact, became the time-honored word that distinguished the sacred writings of the two eras, but aside from that usage it is scarcely heard today. It is true to say that in its early wider use the *berith* stood for any type of contract between two parties. Indeed, its use to describe a sacred divine-human relationship would be a more restricted use of the term. In Ancient Near Eastern culture agreements were made at every turn, in buying and selling, in leases and loans, in the various ways in which we today speak of contracts.

Yet there is good reason for the studied avoidance of the word *contract* to describe the Yahweh-Israel relationship. It is much too legal to highlight the affective dimension of the biblical covenant, and its frequent application to strictly bilateral agreements hardly does justice to the distinctly unequal character and the divine largesse of the Sinai *berith*.

It is *covenant* then that remains in possession, as we attempt to give the expression new life.[2] In modern parlance, *pact* is a word that comes as close as any to what *berith* implies, or what today is referred to as bonding. The latter expression upholds bilateralism, but with the added note of an affective unity. The covenant can never be understood without viewing it in relation to other beliefs of the ancient world. The God of the Hebrews was no deified natural force, nor was this God one of many in a pantheon of deities. Yahweh was not capricious or, even worse, immoral. On the contrary, he was personal, concerned, and engaging. His human involvement is one of design, freely entered into. The step he takes in making an insignificant, nondescript people his very own is what we term a *covenant*.

The Centrality of Sinai. It is against this background, recorded for us in an elaborate form in Exodus 19–24, that the Sinai covenant is to be viewed. As we shall see, the account has been shaped with a variety of overlays in the course of its literary history. But the reason for this is the fact that Sinai stands at the pinnacle of Hebrew faith, flowing as it does into the record of a later history, the exhortations of the prophets, and the poetry of the psalmists. It is in light of the fact that the Hebrews are "dearer to me than all other people" (Ex 19:5) that every event in their history takes on theological importance. Sinai stands at the heart of the Bible and is in a real sense its beginning. In fact, it was in the light of Sinai that the Hebrews looked back upon their earlier history.

It was because of their election at Sinai that questions regarding their past were raised: What is our lineage? Who were our ancestors? Did they have any relationship to this Yahweh who has spoken to us on these mountainous heights? And so the stories of the patriarchs—Abraham, Isaac, and Jacob—came into play. As picture albums stored in the family attic serve as nostalgic links with the past, as pages are turned that evoke memories of a bygone era, and as accomplishments are often embellished in the telling, the stories of Israelite forebears have the ring of folklore. It was out of the Exodus and Sinai experience that Genesis was born. Was not this God already preparing for the covenant in his dealings with the patriarchal families? Abraham was covenanted. The small took precedence over the great. Isaac over Ishmael. Jacob over Esau. Joseph's stay in Egypt brings relief and deliverance to his brothers, the eponymous ancestors of the twelve tribes. These were the stories of people who were important as carriers of the promise.

It was this same Yahweh of Sinai, the primitive "mountain God," who with a strong right hand and a mighty arm had set his people free. The mighty Pharaoh, symbol of the Ancient Near East's imperial grandeur, was rendered impotent and dwarfed to insignificance by a God who was determined to "cast down the mighty and raise up the lowly." In his determination to make of a "no people" a noble people, his sovereignty would become evident. "Deliver us by your wonders, and bring glory to your name" (Dn 3:43). Israel became the carrier of an ongoing promise.

But then a further question rose: Where were we before Abraham? Here religious history reached back into the "twilight zone" of myth and legend to find answers to important questions of origin. Where were we? We were in abysmal darkness, the night of rebellion and waywardness. The story of this nebulous past was told in the ancient traditions of a universal flood, monstrous giants who roamed the earth, homicidal beginnings of brother against brother, pride-constructed towers that reached up to heavenly "no gods." But even in this ugly quagmire of evil, God was present, working toward that dawn of a new era when Abraham would be called from his homeland to follow a new path.

Sin has center stage in our religious prehistory as recorded in the first eleven chapters of Genesis. The primeval revolt in Eden, Cain and Abel, Noah and his disdainful sons, the flood, the ill-begotten giants, the pride of Babel, all play a part in this saga of sin. But it was not always so. In the beginning, as order comes out of chaos, there is nothing but good, serenity, and peace. Covenant actually begins early in Genesis as Yahweh, in a sense, covenants himself with humankind in placing the initial pair in circumstances that in the language of myth were a paradise, an Eden, an idyllic garden. The message is clear. If evil abounds, it is not God's doing. The shadow side of the created order is of human making. This is what the covenanted people of Israel want to affirm in their book of origins. By retrojection, the first chapters of Genesis, which speak of an era when harmony reigned supreme, are the analogous account of a covenant between God and humanity from the start.

In looking at the history of Israel from Sinai onward, that history is meaningless without covenant. Burned searingly into the Israelite psyche, the "bond" was the prism through which the history of the "elect of God" was viewed. It served as the yardstick to measure human conduct. Moral and civil uprightness only had meaning because of their covenant roots. The few successes and the many failures of the kings of Judah and Israel emerge in terms of covenant observance or nonobservance. Even before the monarchy it is around the covenant that tribal federation finds its unity. Without Sinai there would have been no reason for prophetic oracles, the practical teachings of wisdom, or the hymnic praise and lament of the psalter. It comes as no surprise that when the final era is envisioned in post-exilic thought, it is seen as the day of a new covenant.

COVENANT AND HISTORY

What happened at Sinai? Paradoxically it is because the Sinai experience, as recorded in the book of Exodus, was so central to Israelite faith that considerable difficulties are present in trying to unearth the historical nucleus. The event follows the escape of the Israelites from Egypt and their passage through the Red (Reed) Sea and comes to us in its highly elaborate form in Exodus 19–24. The literary account itself reflects a lengthy period of composition, with particularly strong liturgical influences. In fact, the account tells us more about later law, custom, and ritual than it does about the historical event itself.

If one reasons with the biblical text alone, there is a very well-ordered presentation of events from the Exodus to the possession of the land of Canaan. The same group of people constitutes the players in the entire drama. Yet a nagging question remains: Was it all so neat and tidy? Does all the evidence, both biblical and non-biblical, corroborate the Exodus transcript.

Some of the best biblical minds of this century have worked to unravel the actual historical sequence. In looking at the liturgical evidence Gerhard von Rad noted that creedal formulas, reciting God's saving acts on behalf of his people in the passage from Egypt to the land of promise, made no mention of the covenant at Sinai (Dt 26; Jos 24; Ex 15). Von Rad posed the hypothesis of distinct traditions, some involving Sinai, others the Exodus experience, which were merged only with the passage of time. Might it not be that different groups with diverse experiences only brought this together in an organic and literary unity at a later date? The fact that the present text of Exodus sees deliverance, covenant, and land possession as a single unified experience does not mean that it necessarily occurred that way.[3]

This then led to other questions. If the Sinai tradition represents a fusion of different traditions, at what point can we speak of any real national identity? Martin Noth argued that it was in the twelfth and eleventh centuries B.C., after settlement in Canaan and before the monarchy, that the Israelite people as such began to take shape. This was a period of tribal federation composed of various semi-nomadic peoples who found their center in the cult of Yahweh grouped in geographical units connected with the sons of Jacob (the twelve tribes of Israel). As these people united they brought with them their own "God experiences," which were eventually joined in the continuous narrative of the single God who had been both liberator and covenant partner.[4]

The works of both Noth and von Rad were landmark studies that turned important new ground. Today, it is safe to say, their conclusions have been rejected in some instances and qualified in others, even while recognizing the importance of their contribution. It is, for example, difficult to detach completely the Exodus and Sinai when the name of Moses in some of the earliest documentation is closely linked with both events. Furthermore, it can be argued that creedal formulas that litany God's action in favor of his people in moving from Egypt to Canaan need not include the covenant at Sinai, which was basically Israel's response to Yahweh's favor.

For similar reasons, Noth's conclusions are contested as being too categorical. As has been said, the social organization and literary productivity of the twelfth century B.C., while certainly formidable, cannot exclude the living traditions, oral and written, which preceded it. Much of this certainly centered on the Exodus-Sinai experience. In addition, there are various factors that account for the assimilation of new people in Canaan. There is general agreement today that Canaan was not simply overrun and occupied by Israelite invaders. What is presented in the book of Joshua as a blitzkrieg occupation was actually a much more complicated affair. There was a gradual assimilation of people living in the land for a variety of reasons. Some of these could have been nomadic people who had never gone into Egypt; others were absorbed into the Hebrew population because of cultural kinship. Still others may have been Canaanites who rebelled against the Palestinian city-states.[5]

All of this should not distract us from our primary concern in recognizing the fashioning effect that the covenant played in Israelite history. Our discussion, presented here in a simplified form, highlights the difficulties involved in presenting a strictly historical picture. The fact that the text has an organic unity cannot hide the truth that we are dealing with some genuine historical and literary complexities. But, regardless of how it evolved, it is clear that the biblical narrative presents a God who was both deliverer and partner, the Yahweh of the Exodus and Sinai. It is this belief that has become canonized in sacred writings.

A CORE BELIEF

What emerges from this summary review of the evidence is the fact that covenant is a core belief in the Judeo-Christian tradition. What constituted this people as a people was not ethnicity or blood ties but the realization that their origins were transcendent. They had been called together and favored by a deity—known variously as El Shaddai, Elohim, Yahweh, but always as the God of the covenant. In short, the Sinai experience, whatever it may have historically entailed, was for Israel an organizing moment. Like a galaxy of stars revolving around a central planet, considerations of history, ethics, or government could never divorce them from this central consideration. Through the eyes of *berith* the oral and literary custodians of tradition looked to the past and the future. The patriarchs were important because through them Yahweh was preparing the way. With the monarchy in place, after a lengthy weighing of pros and cons, the norms by which the effectiveness of the king's rule was measured were moral and covenant centered. The laws by which the people lived were contained in Torah, the sacred expression of the Lord's will. The plaintive cry of the prophet makes sense only in light of the unique status of the people whom he addressed.

It is vitally important to retain sight of the core belief. It was

9

important then and now. As the organizing moment for Israel was Sinai, so the death and resurrection of Jesus are for Christians. Our problems arise when we fail to set priorities on our beliefs and they all blend together. We recite the creed with great regularity, but that is not to say that each article is of equal value. Core beliefs are those around which other tenets gravitate and have significance. Without the core belief the ancillary features of the creed have no significance at all. Even the norms of conduct find their raison d'être in the fundamental truth by which their importance and gravity are determined. Without a clear notion of the central belief we finish with a religion of observance, without really understanding the why of it all.

The heart of the Jewish-Christian creed lies in the fortuitous juncture of the divine and the human. The worlds of God and humanity are not dichotomous. Through an unparalleled divine initiative, a creating God determined to become part of that creation. There was a plan to be unfolded, and it was to be expressed in the language of God himself. There was no inherent necessity from either side for Sinai to take place. The fact that it did showed incredible favor and goodness on the side of divinity and conferred a remarkable dignity on humanity. This people, a surly band to be sure, and often marked by a lack of appreciation, was henceforth to be identified as "elect," "sacred," "my people." Christianity carries the whole theme forward as God actually "enfleshes" himself in humanness to bring a people home. He "pitched his tent among us" (Jn 1:14b). Again God outdoes himself in generosity, and through the communication of a Spirit, God becomes Abba with the people becoming his family.

This then is the organizing moment. Only when those core beliefs are kept in mind and articulated can there be effective preaching, organic teaching, and a truly motivated living. The covenant of either Testament can never be seen as simply another truth; it is far too pivotal for that. And this prioritization must be a starting point for conversations among confessions. In its decree on ecumenism, the Second Vatican Council states: "When comparing doctrines, theologians should remember that in Catholic teaching there exists an order or 'hierarchy,' since they vary in their relationship to the foundation of the Christian faith."[6] To be persuaded of this statement is to realize that on the core belief there is little that divides us as Christians and, with reference to Sinai, much that unites us with our Jewish partners in the faith. It is from that starting point that subsidiary beliefs proceed. If the rules of conduct, especially the life issues, are deeply rooted in the sacredness of the person, in the design of the God of life for a renewed humanity, then our arguments become much more persuasive. It is only because so much of what we do and say is detached from the core that it is simply labeled as another Christian position. Moreover, our study of covenant will have much to say about community. If we are not to be reduced to sociological considerations only, then it is the espousal of a people, a group, a community in both Testaments that must be kept in mind. Liturgy, doctrine, and ethics all coalesce around covenant as the core belief.

THE LANGUAGE OF COVENANT

Any language about God must be seen as partial and provisional. "At present we see indistinctly as in a mirror, but then face to face. At present I know partially; then I shall know fully, as I am fully known" (1 Cor 13:12). When it came to expressing the relationship between a God who was totally "other," enveloped in mystery, and a people taken as his own, words fell desperately short. The present account of covenant making (Ex 19–24) is encased in layers of descriptive language. Worship has certainly played a part in the fashioning of these chapters, as we shall have occasion to see. They contain, as well, one of Israel's earliest law codes. At one time in the last half-century there was considerable discussion about the role that ancient treaties between countries played in the composition of Exodus 19–24.[7] Once we had a working knowledge through archeological discovery of the way governments dealt with each other, especially when a greater authority cast a mantle of protection over a lesser one, certain similarities were seen with the way the covenant between God and his people was expressed. While the direct influence of the treaty form on the construction of the biblical narrative in Exodus has been largely discredited today,[8] its influence has been felt in other places where the covenant is described, and in its general outline it could very well have had a certain bearing on Exodus. In other words, there was a variety of accepted ways in which agreement between parties was reached, and it would be surprising if this was in no way reflected in Israel's attempt to express this unique relationship. In the course of time, other images served as well. Father and son, husband and wife, king and subjects, shepherd and sheep—all spoke of the same reality, and all admittedly were approximations. Yet there is no escaping the fact that the underlying reality was the core of Israelite faith. In some way the wide chasm between a God of mystery and otherness and a very ordinary people had been bridged. Whatever enlightening image helped to convey that message would not be overlooked.

The Role of Cult. One of the layers of meaning found in the Exodus covenant narrative is rooted in Israel's worship. If we can presume that the covenant was ritualized in cultic ceremonies, eventually centered in the temple, then it is logical to believe that its expression in the Bible would have drawn on these lived experiences. As the eucharistic narratives in the New Testament are more closely associated with the way particular churches were celebrating the liturgical "death of the Lord" than with the actual events of the Last Supper, the same can be said of the Exodus narrative. The way the covenant was commemorated has played a considerable part in the way the event has come down to us.

Was there an annual ceremony of covenant renewal in Israel's liturgical life? The Bible itself is silent about the question, although there were certainly major moments in which the people solemnly recommitted themselves to the covenant relationship (Jos 24; Neh 9–10). Many of the psalms may well be situated in such a ceremony, which is often identified with the annual feast of Tents. There is, nonetheless, one indisputable fact: the Sinai tradition as we have received it bears a strong liturgical imprint. A careful analysis of chapters 19–24 bears this out. What are the basic components? Initially Yahweh invites and the people respond favorably (chap. 19), the terms of the agreement are set forth (chap. 20), and there is a solemn acceptance and ratification (chap. 24). The law code in chapters 21–23 is a later addition and is easily excised without disturbing the flow of the account. Now it is within this basic framework that the liturgical motif repeatedly emerges. Certainly it is retrojection from a much later date, but so is a great deal of the legislation of Leviticus, much of it ill fitted to the nomadic life of a desert existence.

A few examples will help. There are shades of the temple sanctuary as the mountaintop is declared "off limits" to all except Moses and Aaron (Ex 19:12). A further line of demarcation prevents any clerical or lay ascent of the mountain, or even touching it (19:12, 24). Ritual purity is called for, with a temporary prohibition of sexual intercourse and a washing of garments (19:14f.). A hierarchy of groups becomes quite pronounced prior to the covenant's ratification. Moses comes closest to God (the high priest), with the priests and elders at a distance (temple personnel), and the people farther removed (24:1f.). Sacrificial rites, the construction of the altar and memorial pillars, the sacred meal, the stylized verbal formulas are all features that go beyond historical data and reflect a variety of liturgical customs. In a sense, Sinai has become the temple itself, where the glory of the Lord is manifest (24:16). It is there that sacrifice is appropriately situated and any ceremony of covenant renewal would find its logical setting.

WORSHIP AND THE STORY

There is an obvious conclusion at this point in our study of covenant; this conclusion is more than an interesting parenthesis. For Israel, worship was rooted in the events of history. It is not the endless cycles of natural forces or feasts centered wholly on seasons of the year that are to the fore. The culture that surrounded early Israel centered on appeasing or satisfying the deified forces of fertility. But Israelite prayer evolved around the story. The saving event was ritualized. Those events that centered on a God of mystery were constantly relived in prayer, whether in the temple, the family circle, or in solitude.

It is interesting to note that the retelling of the Exodus story in cult was actually cast in the mold of pre-existing pastoral and agricultural feasts, connected with the subduing and stabilization of nature. Both the feasts of Passover and Unleavened Bread, which center on the deliverance from Egyptian bondage under

Pharaoh, were originally feasts connected with pasturing the flocks and cultivating grain among semi-nomadic and agrarian Near Eastern people. The killing of the prized lamb in the light of the springtime's full moon was an offering of gratitude and supplication to the appropriate deity. In addition, the offering of the first grain of the season in a pure and incorrupt state was an important sign of allegiance.[9]

As these feasts are historicized in Israel, the slain lamb becomes the paschal victim, whose sprinkled blood is a preservative against death by the avenging angel. Celebrated with loins girt, sandaled feet, and staff in hand (Ex 12), the feast is reminiscent of its pastoral origins, although the symbolism is now one of a hurried departure. For seven days the unleavened bread of a swift leave-taking was to be a reminder of the bitterness and harshness of the lengthy stay in Egypt. Thus ritual and symbol told the story in a very living and concrete way. "When your children ask you,'What does this rite of yours mean?'" symbol becomes catechesis.

A form of liturgical replay of saving events is captured vividly in the final pages of the book of Joshua (chap. 24). Yahweh's deliverance starts with the patriarchs and moves through Moses and Aaron, the Exodus, the desert journey, and the possession of the land (vv. 2–13). Following this litany of favor, there is the proposal of the covenant terms calling for the people's acceptance or rejection (vv. 14f.), followed by a four-times-repeated collective expression of consent to the covenant terms (vv. 16–24). The act is solemnly remembered with the setting up of the memorial stone (vv. 25–27). This covenant at Shechem, a site never occupied or seized, may well recall what was historically the incorporation of Canaanite people, inhabitants of the land prior to the Israelite incursion. In its present developed form it becomes a credo of belief in which history and cult coalesce.

THE BOND OF LOVE

Our understanding of covenant has deep roots in legal agreements in antiquity that regulated relations between individuals, groups, and nations. As such, they lent stability to all levels of society. But the language of biblical covenant is not exhausted by the language of law. The covenant springs from the totally free initiative of a God who desires engagement. The human response to that initiative, as Deuteronomy repeatedly states, is to be one of gratitude and love.

The vocabulary of covenant is very revealing in pointing up certain divine and human attributes at the heart of the relationship. *Righteousness,* for example, or *to be righteous,* in its basic understanding means to stand on the side of truth. Yahweh was righteous when he was supportive of Israel's concerns, as when he fought for Israel against its foes. This made him savior or liberator. But just as the notion of salvation evolved so too did righteousness. The covenant itself was a major salvific act, and Yahweh's concern for this insignificant and disenfranchised people underscored his righteousness. This led to conclusions about the constancy and stability of God: he was not capricious or whimsical. Humans were not pawns on some terrestrial chess border. God was seen as righteous because he could not be otherwise, and it was experience, not abstract speculation, that brought that truth home.

The love of God then becomes covenant love *(hesed).* This word coupled with fidelity *(emeth)* appears again and again in the prophets and the psalms as eloquently expressive of the sentiments connected with the bond. It was God's *hesed* that prompted his initial outreach in drawing a people to himself. It is his unflagging fidelity that makes him stand by the agreement, even in the face of flagrant violations and repeated failure. One is forced to ask if these qualities of covenant love and fidelity were disclosed in that glimpse of God "from behind" promised Moses in Exodus (chap. 33). At least it is interesting to note that in the subsequent chapter Yahweh identifies himself as the One who is "merciful and gracious...rich in kindness *(hesed)* and fidelity *(emeth)*" (Ex 34:6). The point is this: the covenant gave these words their meaning; without it such qualities would have been nothing more than a matter of speculation. Eventually it is *hesed* that is seen to be at work in all of Yahweh's activity, destined as it was for Israel's benefit. And so Psalm 136 can litany the acts of God's *hesed,* which extend from creation

15

(vv. 4–9) through all the events of the Exodus, even those that spelled death and disaster for Israel's foes.

What is to be the response of a grateful people? The same spirit of *hesed* and *emeth*. This affective dimension of the covenant expresses its significance. It was this love relationship that was so characteristic of Israel's youth, the desert years to which the prophets hearken back (Jer 2:2). It carried the connotation of thankfulness, faithfulness, and loyalty. In fact, it is these very qualities that give meaning to law. Israel's oldest law codes, the decalogue (Ex 20:2–17) and the covenant code (Ex 21–23), find their literary setting within the framework of covenant making. Law observance, in the past as well as today, can never be separated from its inherent relationship with God's protective and saving action.[10]

"YES" TO A CARING GOD

We have spent some time on the complexities of the covenant tradition. It can be argued that whether or not the Exodus and Sinai tradition was experienced as a unity is not a question of major moment in our understanding of the biblical message. What is important is the way in which the narrative as a whole thrusts the Exodus God to the fore as the principal actor. This overwhelming sense of outreach, of God's generosity and concern, emerges in bold relief. This is not a God to be sought, a disengaged "other" reality, separate and aloof. Rather, it is a God who wants to "save" even in the act of creating. Those mighty acts of the Exodus, as culturally conditioned as they were, bringing both deliverance and destruction, are all refracted through the prism of a caring God.

Thus, when Yahweh asks for a response marked by observance and fidelity, it is only in the light of benefits experienced. When a grateful people asks itself, What is the appropriate response?, the answer is clear: "Be holy, for I, the LORD your God, am holy" (Lv 19:2). Human conduct becomes a concrete expression of the otherness of Yahweh. And therein lies the authentic role of law in our religious tradition. When the law is detached from gratitude, when covenant response is detached from the benefits of the Exodus, then morality is akin to acquiring athletic prowess. To arrive at a determined goal is a question of trying perseverance, the arduous pursuit of determined skills. Much of the literature on "acquiring perfection" in an earlier era set it forth in just those terms. It was wearisome, uninspiring, and dotted with guilt-ridden setbacks. It is only love that makes it all worthwhile; if covenant teaches us nothing more than that, it has succeeded.

We do not give sufficient attention to the part that experience plays in the Judeo-Christian tradition. This is not a deity who is primarily involved in explaining why things happen. Many questions are left unanswered. The impact that the Exodus made on the faith of Israel is inestimable, fashioning, as it did, a two-thousand-year history. Events spoke, stories cast their spell. In the light of the Exodus and Sinai, patriarchal family history became important, as did the "twilight zone" of prehistory. Later events continued to tell the story as God touched human lives in the occupation of the land, the tragedy of foreign invasion, deportation, and restoration. This was not a faith wrapped in the interminable cycles of nature or accepted as a panacea for realities that defy human explanation. It is a history with a beginning and a determined end. No term could better describe the human component than *people of God*. It is on the world stage of history with all its glories and tragedies that this story unfolds.

If the modern Jews see themselves as people of the land, one can at least understand the reason for their stance. Unfortunately, historical circumstances have altered the Palestinian picture, and political problems of present-day Palestine cannot be solved solely on theological grounds. But geographical identity was much more deeply seen as a focal point of unity for the Jews than Rome ever became for the Catholic world. If anything ever approximated a theocracy, Israel did, wherein families, tribes, and nation found their raison d'être in God. It is not the bonds of blood or natural kinship that forge a people but the response to a divine call, the willingness to say yes to a single God. There can be little doubt that the book of Joshua is schematic, and the occupation of the land was more a question of assimilation than conquest. Over time, greater numbers of nomadic, semi-nomadic, and settled people accepted this covenant God. It was truly a faith-formed community.

It is this drama played out on the world stage of history that gives Judeo-Christianity such a uniqueness. We are not indifferent to world events, nor do we view them from some lofty Mount Olympus. Indeed, history has played a vital part in faith understanding. In the incursions of Assyria, Babylon, Greece, and Rome, God's hand was seen at work in a reading of "the signs of the times." There are questions to be asked about the events of history, and they are questions that touch our belief. They extend from the crusades and the holy wars to the rise and fall of the Soviet empire and, yes, to the Holocaust. There are no easy answers, but they are questions with which faith must wrestle. However, the starting point is the fact that God is part of history. Having bonded with a people, God can never be separated from the human adventure.

God of the covenant, I am grateful for your presence in history and for the love you have shown your people. We did not discover you; no, you discovered us. Your covenant reminds us that as weak and frail as we are, you desperately want to be our God. Thank you for calling us to yourself through Abraham, Moses, Joshua, and above all, through Jesus, who shows us the way to you and who lives with you forever. Amen.

FOR STUDY AND DISCUSSION

1. In its biblical sense what does the term *covenant* mean? Is the word understood today, or should we search for a substitute?
2. How would you describe the importance of the covenant in understanding the Bible? Why do we speak of it as a core belief?
3. The Bible presents the Exodus-covenant-desert period and occupation of Canaan as a continuous series of events. Is such necessarily the case? Discuss the pros and cons.
4. Discuss the liturgical imprint on the Sinai narrative (Ex 19–24).
5. The divine attributes of covenant love *(hesed)* and fidelity *(emeth)* are repeatedly linked with the Sinai event. Explain their significance.
6. The covenant was Israel's response to a gracious God. Explain the importance of this concept in any biblical theology of the Old Testament.

2

THE COVENANT AND LAW

"Come to me, all you that yearn for me,
  and be filled with my fruits;...
He who eats of me will hunger still,
  he who drinks of me will thirst for more;...
All this is true of the book of the Most High's covenant,
  the law which Moses commanded us." (Sir 24:18, 20, 22)

Two Franciscan friars were once discussing a superior who exercised considerable control over their lives in a former era. The comment of one was: "Old Joe was strict but kind." Replied the other: "We never had any trouble finding his strictness." When it comes to our institutional faith as Catholics we often feel a similar ambivalence in speaking of law and love. In an earlier era love was much talked about, but we never had trouble finding the law. We began by learning the commandments and then built our moral life around precepts, carefully distinguishing between transgressions that were mortal and those that were venial. The examination of conscience, which always preceded that rather frightening and mysterious encounter in the confessional, looked into the "nooks and crannies" of our daily life to see how far we had wandered. All of this may well have been meant to center on the Good Shepherd, the benevolent father of the prodigal son, or whatever biblical image of compassion one might choose, but it was still, to a considerable extent, a religion of observance.

The Importance of Law. Law is an absolute necessity for the human community. Its presence is simply a given in our daily life; its absence from civil society would spell chaos. That it is an important part of the God-human relationship is perfectly logical, not only because much of religious legislation is for the good of society as a whole, but also because it spells allegiance to the divine Source of all good. What is important and extremely precarious is the balancing act that must keep law in subordination to love. If such is successful, then we are dealing with a heartfelt expression of gratitude. If it fails, then we end up with the type of legal Pharisaism that Jesus deplored.

Law played an important part in the covenant with Israel, and the present chapter will look at its content. But just as the covenant law code was situated at the heart of the covenant being fashioned in Exodus 19–24, we cannot consider the precepts that governed Israelite life apart from the bonding in love that undergirds them and gives them meaning.

When we examine the laws found in the covenant code (chapters 20:22–23:19), we are looking at Israel's oldest code. In its present context it is preceded by the decalogue (chap. 20), which as a comprehensive summary of the norms of human conduct stands in a class by itself.

In Israel, as distinguished from many cultures of the times, the law was given by the deity and its observance marked by adherence to his moral will. At the same time the good of society was inextricably linked to the religious response. What makes the decalogue so unique is the extent to which it embraces human dealings with God and with others in a way that leaves no significant dimension of that relationship untouched. Proceeding from there to the other law codes of the Pentateuch, there is cultic and social legislation that touched on the various aspects of life—property, finances, marriage, ritual purity, and temple worship. Laws were either general in character (apodictic) or based on cases (casuistic).[1] The former have a broad sweeping character and are meant to be all-inclusive ("You shall...You shall not"), as in the decalogue; the latter cite the circumstances and the accompanying sanctions ("When a person..." "If a person..."). While many of these laws find a parallel in other cultures, they are brought together here and rooted in the human response to Yahweh's will and therefore have a sacred character. If this dimension is lost sight of, religious law becomes an end in itself, altering its intended meaning.

20

This is nowhere more clearly seen than in the work of the Deuteronomist, who in his "book of the law" places law clearly at the service of love. The great *Shema'*, the basic credo of Hebrew prayer, emphasizes Yahweh as the sole deity and the role of law as a response of love. "Hear, O Israel! The LORD is our God, the LORD alone! Therefore, you shall love the LORD, your God, with all your heart and with all your soul, and with all your strength" (Dt 6:4f.). The exhortation to a heartfelt response permeates Deuteronomy. Later experience was to illustrate how much law observance apart from love gave religious faith a distinctly different character.[2]

When we speak of social and theological development within Israel, there is no underestimating the importance of the period that followed the Babylonian exile in the sixth century. The historical climate and the events it embraced conditioned the faith response of the people in a number of very significant ways. The era of the actual exile was a historical and theological watershed. Far from their homeland, without the temple and all it signified, with much of their traditional distinctiveness lost, Israel became increasingly the "people of the book." The period after the exile can be best described as one of feverish literary activity, with the writing, compiling, and editing of a lengthy sacred tradition. It was then that the Bible as we know it began to take shape. With the ascendancy of the role of the high priest as a religious and civil authority, the law is accorded an exalted and singular character in the life of the community. After resettlement in Jerusalem, Ezra gives it a solemn reading at a major convocation of the people (Neh 8). In the centuries that followed, the law served a dominant role in the formation of the people. It was interpreted and commented upon extensively; its observance was the measure of the faithful Jew; and countless precepts had been attached to it. By the dawn of the Christian era the legalism against which Jesus inveighs was very much to the fore.

THE DECALOGUE

It is safe to say that in years past if a Catholic schoolchild learned anything it was the Ten Commandments. This was usually done

prior to first confession, and from that point on the commandments served as the handy "rule-of-thumb" for measuring our
moral responses and determining our culpability. Whatever may
be said for or against a "decalogue morality," there is no doubt
about the fact that the commandments served as a unique com-
pendium of moral behavior and facilitated the "tracking" that had
to be done.

The origins of the decalogue are to be found in the early
stages of Israel's Sinai tradition. It appears twice in the Pentateuch, once in Exodus (20:1–17), and once in Deuteronomy
(5:6–21). It may well have been the original body of laws connected with Sinai; it was later relocated in the text by the addition
of the covenant code (Ex 21–23) and placed in its present rather
awkward position. As the text now stands, Moses descends from
the mountain to speak to the people (19:20), at which point the
decalogue is unexpectedly introduced (20:1–17). The narrative
regarding Moses and the people then resumes (vv. 18–21).
Moses returns to the mountain for another exchange with the
Lord, at which point the covenant code is introduced. It is clear
from the uneven character of the text that the decalogue was
moved forward to make room for the covenant code, only adding
to the ample evidence for a conflated text, something not foreign to Exodus 19–24 as a whole. The decalogue in Exodus is
part of the Elohist tradition and differs in secondary ways from
its Deuteronomic counterpart.[3]

In Christian circles we are quite accustomed to the rather all-
embracing character of the decalogue. It may come as a surprise
to some that the Hebrew understanding of the "ten words" differs from our own. Christian tradition built on the primitive
understanding and broadened the understanding of what the
precepts envisioned. The decalogue begins with Yahweh's
solemn self presentation: "I, the LORD, am your God, who
brought you out of the land of Egypt, that place of slavery" (Ex
20:2). It is very important that it not only introduces the lawgiver
but links him with the saving action of the Exodus. If this is an
early text and considered primitive, then the view that would see
the Exodus and the covenant as the experience of separate and
distinct groups finds itself in difficulty. The link between the two

events is very clear here. This would point to a juncture of Exodus and covenant, liberation and engagement, grace and law.

The Commandments Directly Related to God. The first three commandments are God centered and deal with the proper moral posture vis-à-vis the deity. The first precept calls for a very exclusive monotheistic worship (20:3f.): in any cultic setting ("before my face"), the veneration of any other god is excluded. It is a practical rather than a speculative statement regarding the existence of other deities. Yahweh, in short, admits no competitors. One may wonder whether or not there was the admission of the existence of other gods. Since they were not to be reckoned with or accorded any status, it was of little consequence to consider whether or not other gods existed. For all practical purposes they were "no gods"; where there was no recognition, there was no divinity. Moreover, "you shall not carve idols." Israelite faith was also non-iconic; no images of Yahweh or, needless to say, other deities were permitted. This underscores the totally "other" nature of Yahweh; further, in antiquity deities were so intimately connected with their images that any form of localization could easily lead to a sense of control or domination.

The concept of the sacred imposed clear limitations on any cultic expression. In the course of time Yahweh's name became unutterable in Hebrew society. Such was not the original meaning of the decalogue's second precept (20:7). The actual commandment envisions any improper use of the name, whether in false oaths, cursing, or magic incantation (Lv 19:12). This is much a part of how the ancients envisioned the connection between the person and the name. In knowing a person's name, I have acquired unusual access to his personal domain. Knowledge of the name signified power over the one so designated; to give a name fixed his or her destiny. While Yahweh's name is disclosed to Moses, even though enigmatically (Ex 3:14), restrictions were placed on its use and eventually it was not spoken at all, with *Lord* used instead.

The origins of the sabbath are shrouded in obscurity. It was always a characteristic feature of Hebrew life, and exact parallels in other cultures are not easily come by. As the third precept of the decalogue (20:8–11), it would seem that primitively it provided rest from the toil of daily life. From a theological standpoint it was a reminder of human dependence on God. It was to be a day of total rest, with all forms of work excluded (Ex 31:12–17), even building a fire (Ex 35:3). Motivation for its observance is given in two forms. In Exodus it is a reminder of what Yahweh himself did after the work of creation in six days was terminated. In Deuteronomy it is connected with the arduous ordeal of the life in Egypt (Dt 5:12–15). Primarily, however, like the observance of the sabbatical year and the jubilee, the sabbath was a reminder of the true source of life. The ability to stand back and reflect on providence was a reminder of human insufficiency and divine largesse. In Israel there was no cultic observance connected with the sabbath.

The Commandments Related to Others. The remaining precepts of the decalogue regulate human relationships, specifically those within the Israelite community itself. First consideration goes to parents, who were not only the transmitters of life but of tradition as well. Just as they brought the child to physical and religious maturity, the offspring had responsibilities to them as the aging process set in. This obedience and respect due to parents was life long, not restricted to one's younger years (Ex 21:17; Lv 20:9; Dt 21:18–21).

In setting priorities for the goods of human existence, primacy is given to life itself. The fifth commandment forbids killing, whether voluntary or involuntary; it is directed against homicide and manslaughter. The verb "to kill" (Hebr: *rasah*), which is used here, looks to the helpless condition of the victim. In fact, in Deuteronomy this type of murder is compared to the violation of a girl in an open field, in an isolated place far from the town where any form of assistance is unavailable. The accent is on total helplessness (Dt 22:25f.). Thus the precept does not deal with killing in war or suicide.

After his own well-being, a person's family ranks highest on the list of his concerns. As difficult as it may be for us to come to grips with Hebrew thought in our much more woman-conscious world, we have to admit that it is the rights of the man that are protected by the sixth commandment. In a strongly patriarchal society, the woman was a part of a man's property and is frequently listed among his holdings (Ex 20:17). Thus, adultery could be committed by a man or a woman, but it was a violation of another man's rights (Lv 20:10; Dt 22:22). For this reason the law did not look to the case of sexual relations between a man and an unmarried woman, unless she was the daughter of a priest. The law has its parallels in Assyrian and Babylonian legal codes. Since engagement was solemn and established legal rights even before cohabitation, the precept applied to that state as well.

Most people would be surprised to learn that originally it was not theft that was prohibited by "you shall not steal" but kidnapping; material goods are protected by the last precept of the decalogue (Ex 20:17). Here it is the deprivation of a person's freedom or freedom of movement, through abduction, arrest, or enforced slavery, that is prohibited. The penalty for such a crime is death (Ex 21:16).

The "bearing of false witness" in the eighth precept looks to official judicial procedures. What is called for in public testimony here, as in the code of Hammurabi, is absolute truth. The danger of an erroneous or unjust sentence, especially in capital cases, was real, and every effort was taken to uphold the truth. The witness of one person only was not sufficient (Nm 35:30; Dt 19:15–21).

The "coveting" prohibited by the final commandment (divided into two in the Catholic decalogue) says much more than simple desire; the Hebrew verb *hamad* implies an initiative to realize the desired end. Forbidden is any *attempt* to appropriate the goods (household) of another man, ranging from his wife to his livestock and material possessions.

THE DECALOGUE AND HUMAN VALUES

After attempting to understand the decalogue in its original cultural and religious context, we are probably inclined to ask how the church got so much more out of the commandments than was originally intended. The question is a valid one, and in some cases we seem to have drained them to the last drop. Any morality of precepts has inherent dangers, if we stop with the precepts or if the precepts become too numerous. But there are positive things to be said about the decalogue that cannot be lost sight of in our modern age.

The lack of respect for life in our century has reached staggering proportions. Bloodshed has stained the entire fabric of modern civilization. Life is cheap and is considered such—in massive violations of human rights, national issues solved through massive bloodshed, drug wars with drive-by shootings, retaliation through senseless bombings and terrorizing the innocent, the taking of life in the womb and at the twilight of human existence. Never was all of this made more macabre and grotesque than when the assailant of passengers on a New York commuter train became his own lawyer at his trial and cross-examined his victims on the stand.

In all of this there is a wanton disregard for the human person. The inherent worth of the person is the basic and universal precept that stands out in the decalogue. There is a deep sense of human dignity in a cultural milieu that often dismissed human life as a matter of little consequence. The genius of the Israelite tradition, whose major contribution to world civilization has always been seen as religious, is its remarkable understanding of God and the value of the individual in God's sight. And so the decalogue ranges over the whole spectrum of life's concern. Aging parents, the right to safety and security, the inviolable character of the marriage relationship, human freedom, and personal property are all safeguarded in one of the oldest law codes known to humanity.

The timeless character of the decalogue is centered in respect for the most fundamental values in human society. And while modernity may well pride itself on its many accomplishments, the sad fact is that the failure to recognize "decalogue morality" plagues our life today. This not only means that our technologically developed society still finds itself incapable of dealing effectively with deadly crime, homelessness, and addiction, but that it has given its blessing to the taking of life in the womb, the death penalty, and has come dangerously close to approving euthanasia.

CHRISTIANITY AND THE DECALOGUE

Christ has transposed the Hebrew ethic to a new key. We are called to go far beyond the requirements of the law. But the teaching of the decalogue always remains the starting point. Not only does it regulate our response to the needs of society, but it expresses the moral will of God, to whom we are ethically responsible. Governments must support and uphold the moral order of society; they are not its custodian, and even less its source. Formation in those life issues of the decalogue looks first to the family and then to the church. And it is precisely there that so much erosion has occurred. Dysfunctional families, latch-key children, and single parenthood are all features of a family life that lacks the "glue" of a former age wherein values were taught and, more especially, lived at home. When the church exercised its strong magnetic pull and the parochial school formed the matrix of moral education, the family was strongly supported in arriving at its goals. Today much of that has vanished. So we are left with a moral vacuum that is reflected in home, church, and society.

We can expect a change for the better when the decalogue, shared by Jew and Christian alike, is authentically integrated into the lives of our young. We are fully aware that in the Christian life we do not stop there, but the fact remains that there is no better starting point. Parents and religious leaders can hardly fault civil government for its failures when the first responsibility rests with them. There is a timeless wisdom to be found in those ten basic precepts, and we ignore them only at the risk of continued dissolution of the fabric of our lives as part of the human enterprise.

THE CODE OF THE COVENANT

There is general agreement that the "code of the covenant" (Ex 20:22–23:33) is Israel's earliest attempt to codify its law, soon after the occupation of Canaan. It is largely based on case law, derived from situations arising in daily life, and is in no way exhaustive or comprehensive. In many ways it takes the norms of the decalogue and gives them specific application. For example, the relationship to God issues in concrete norms regarding the altar and sanctuary (20:24–26). The right to life, enshrined in the prohibition of killing, gives rise to a series of laws dealing with personal injury or any serious threat to life (21:12–32). Due respect for another's property, the final precept of the decalogue, is reflected in laws regarding slaves (21:1–11), property

27

damage and theft (21:37—22:4). Admittedly, many of these laws grew out of social need and looked to the good order of society. Yet Israel saw them always as an expression of Yahweh's moral will.

THE HOLINESS CODE

This code stems from the priestly tradition and is weighted in favor of cultic concerns (Lv 17–26). It regulates sacrifice (chap. 17), priesthood (chap. 21), sacred times and seasons (chaps. 23 and 25). Once again the norms that regulate human conduct highlight that singular concern for human dignity which is at the center of covenant life (chaps. 18 and 19).

The repeated refrain "I am the Lord" points to Yahweh himself as the author of the legislation. We are, however, far removed from Moses and the era of his exchange with the Lord. But it was that link with the past that gave force and meaning to all subsequent legislation; the cloak of Mosaic authority raised later law to a level of unquestionable status. That link with tradition was vitally important to belief and practice.

Leviticus, in addition, sees fidelity to law as conduct that reflects the holiness or "otherness" of God. "To me, therefore, you shall be sacred; for I, the LORD, am sacred" (20:26) is a theme that will echo in the Matthean Jesus' injunction in the sermon on the mount (Mt 5:48). One of the primary functions of faith in the Judeo-Christian tradition is to bring God to the world, not solely the world to God. While the universe is his handiwork, the God of our faith tradition remains totally distinct from creation. He cannot be captured or envisioned, apart from Jesus, who is the sole window on God; it is only human conduct, in embodying God's teaching and directives, that makes him present. This God whom "one cannot see and continue to live" becomes visible and experienced in the embrace of law, the expression of his moral will. The code of holiness goes beyond ritual or legal purity, seeing in moral rectitude a reflection of that holiness which defies human comprehension.

THE DEUTERONOMIC CODE

If law ever spoke the language of love, it is in the book of Deuteronomy, the book that had more impact than perhaps any other in Israelite history. While in its final form the book is at least six hundred years younger than Moses, its literary presentation is that of a "second covenant" made with the Hebrews through Moses before taking possession of the land; this covenant is quite distinct from that made on Sinai (Horeb). Its literary structure is strikingly similar to the Near Eastern suzerainty treaties made between major political rulers and lesser powers.

As in the case of the Exodus law code, the laws of Deuteronomy are situated in a covenant framework. Some of the laws repeat what has already been set forth in Exodus, as, for example, the decalogue (Dt 5:6–21), but the most striking feature about Deuteronomy is the extent to which it sees law observance as an expression of love. This is far more than simple adherence to established norms. The love of God has reached Israel in the countless favors received from the time of the Exodus, at Horeb (Sinai), and in the years of the desert sojourn. Now the land of promise is about to be given to them as well. The total commitment requested of Israel can only be measured in terms of love; in fact, the great *Shema'* (6:4f.), one of the Jews' most sacred prayers, centers entirely on the love of the Lord with all of one's natural forces.

Another characteristic of the Deuteronomist is the conditional bilateralism of the agreement. God's love is not so unconditional as to be untempered by his justice. Divine goodness and fidelity will be experienced to the extent that a people chosen and set apart is responsive and observant. This is no warrior-God, almost magically bound to his people; the covenant is freely entered into on the basis of love, and it is a "two-way street," with affective bonds binding each side.

In the late seventh century B.C., during the reign of King Josiah, a "book of the law" was discovered in the temple in the course of renovations (2 Kgs 22). This "miraculous" discovery is presented as a major factor in the reform launched by Josiah, and the book discovered is frequently identified with an early text of

29

Deuteronomy. After its discovery Josiah presided over a ceremony of covenant renewal during which the book's contents
were read aloud in the hearing of the people (2 Kgs 23:1ff.).
Whatever is to be said about the actual book and its contents,
there is no doubting the striking similarities that exist between
features of Josiah's reform and the book of Deuteronomy.

THINKING ABOUT LAW

It is probably safe to say that we have rather ambivalent feelings about law. When it works to our favor, we look upon it
kindly; when it infringes on our freedom, we become a little hostile. A red light at the crossing in front of the school that our children attend receives hearty endorsement. The low speed limit on
a carless four-lane highway extending to the distant horizon
brings out nothing but negative feelings. Yet when all is said and
done, the reasonable person understands the purpose of law in
caring for the common good and is willing to observe it, even
when it is somewhat unpleasant.

Law in a religious context is another matter. While laws are
necessary to direct any organization, there is a rather general
consensus that laws touching on religion should be kept to a minimum. No one would question the reasonable character of the
decalogue, especially when understood in its original Hebrew
setting. It spells out in general terms the norms that should regulate relations with God and neighbor.[4]

LEGALISM

There is always the danger, however, that law can rise to a level
of such prominence that one can hardly see the forest for the
trees. Law can be an effective means of control, a goal that has
not always been alien to authority, whether religious or civil. In
addition, there is something consoling and secure about law
observance. If the road to heaven has unmistakable guardrails,
then we are better assured of reaching our destination. Law can
offer that security. It removes doubt, asks only for conformity,
and gives us the assurance that we want. The Judaism of Jesus'

time was fashioned along those lines, and he took endless issue with it. It was not too many decades ago, certainly within living memory, that more class hours a week in the seminary were devoted to a law-centered moral theology and canon law than to biblical studies. Whatever its readily acknowledged importance, a preponderance of time given to law has that deadening effect that Paul decries. The law kills; the Spirit gives life.

What is striking about the biblical law codes is the extent to which they have been contextualized. It is never a question of establishing norms of conduct, whether related to social, religious, or political life, as an end in itself. Law is always expressive of a relationship, a way of bonding with God, the authentic "yes" to a gracious power. The code of the covenant is precisely that, a series of laws placed within the context of the covenant. Observance springs from the fact that God has first shown concern for his people. If the Exodus experience stands behind the earliest code of law, then law is given a very distinctive framework and a tone that is positive and humanizing. In a sense, the Hebrews would have been deprived and disadvantaged if there had been no way to give a response to God's concern. In some ancient cultures law was not seen as linked with religious observance. Moral uprightness was not necessarily linked with respect for a deity. In fact, many of the gods outdid their human minions in moral depravity and were hardly in a position to legislate morality. Such is clearly not the case in Israel.

What makes the law code of Leviticus so striking in its call to holiness is that it is a reflection of Yahweh himself. With its plethora of detail touching every aspect of life, in ways that are extremely difficult for us to grasp, the priestly law code evidenced the existence of God and in its sense of the sacred told us what kind of God he is. It is when we can see law in that light that it passes from mere acceptance to challenge.

It is small wonder that Deuteronomy had the influence it did. Like the eagle that spreads its wings to carry its young aloft in one of the book's final songs (32:11), the Lord calls his people to the heights in seeing the law as the noblest expression of love, fidelity, and commitment. It is in this book, which predates Christianity by centuries, that Jesus finds the expression that summarizes the ethic of the reign of God—the love of the Lord and him alone.

LAW AS AN EXPRESSION OF LOVE

Law and religion perform a delicate balancing act. We cannot live without law, nor can we live with too much of it. Christianity is above all a religion of motivation, centered in the Spirit. This means there must be sufficient latitude for the Spirit to act, and law should never stifle that inner freedom. Religious authority on any level is well advised to encourage and motivate people rather than turning to legislation. Yet law is always with us, and it is covenant law that makes the most sense. Not only should law be reasonable, but it should be heartily endorsed. It is an avenue for the expression of gratitude to a God who has repeatedly shown his love for us. In a society that gives little thought to the world of the Spirit, the experience of God in a believing community (indeed in a believing person) through the acceptance of God's will has a very distinctive value. The Hebrew covenant has much to teach us. It places law squarely at the center of God's outreach, his willingness to bond with humankind. That makes all the difference in the world.

Let us return to the courtroom. During a major riot in Los Angeles some years ago, a man was pulled from his truck by assailants on one of the main avenues and was severely beaten, almost to the point of death. Months later the trial against the perpetrators took place. Sentencing finally followed and the interests of justice were served. Through it all, however, the man spoke of his forgiveness for those at whose hands he had suffered. His composure and calm seemed almost out of place in a court of law. At the end of the trial he crossed the courtroom and embraced the families of his assailants. It was an incredibly powerful witness to what the gospel teaches. Yes, the interests of the law had been served. But the law and the Spirit call us to go further and make God present in the warmth of an embrace.

God of the covenant, you gave us law; now teach us its meaning. In my basic obligations I want to observe what you ask, but always in a spirit of love. I also know that I am called to go beyond any law in my complete love for you and my neighbor. Help me to see both the law and the Spirit as expressions of your love for me, and grant me a spirit willing to respond. Amen.

FOR STUDY AND DISCUSSION

1. In the Bible, law is situated within the context of covenant. Why is that significant?
2. What is the difference between apodictic and casuistic law? Cite examples of each.
3. Explain how the decalogue is a prioritized summary of moral conduct.
4. Compare the Hebrew and Christian understandings of each of the precepts of the decalogue.
5. If we do not live an Old Testament ethic, what is the importance of the decalogue for the Christian life?
6. Identify Israel's three major law codes.
7. Discuss the dangers inherent in according law too dominant a role in the life of faith. Discuss the importance of contextualizing law.
8. Cite examples of love taking precedence over law.

3

Covenant Before and After Sinai

"Think back on the days of old, reflect on the years of age upon age. Ask your father and he will inform you, ask your elders and they will tell you." (Dt 32:7)

Memory and hope. Both our human and religious experiences are rooted in that which has happened and that which is to come. And unfortunately much is overlooked in the interests of the present. As I began work a number of years ago in a Catholic seminary on the east coast, an auxiliary bishop of the diocese we served was speaking to me of my work at his alma mater. Yes, he noted, most priests ordained from there have good and bad memories and feel warmth and coolness, or both. But, he said, the students should never forget that they are part of a great tradition. Yet that was probably the very thing we thought of least in our concern with tomorrow's exam, the inadequacies of students or professors, liturgical responsibilities, and the quality of the food. The fact is that we are all part of a tradition, heirs of a patrimony. Yet, how seldom we think of the history of our neighborhood, our city, our firm, our parish.

It is that link with the past that paves the way for the future. We are increasingly a people without hope. In this crime-infested world what will be the future of our children? What is there to live for? The answer is more positive than we expect if we recognize all that our forebears had to surmount. These may not be the best of times, but who is to say that they are the worst? If we live only in the present, then there is nothing ahead of us but the cold nuclear winter. It is only when we have one arm extended to the past and the other to the future that we attain the balance we desire.

Nowhere do memory and hope play a stronger role than in our faith experience. The desert people with Moses looked back to Egypt and forward to Canaan. Daniel the visionary saw former political powers crumble while the Hebrews survived. Jesus looked forward to drinking the new wine in the kingdom of God even as he asked that a sacred repast be repeated in his memory.

In the present chapter we will see how the covenant served as the linchpin between the past and future. If contemporary biblical research has established anything, it is the fact that the past and future were viewed through the prism of the actual event, giving all three points on the temporal line a very distinctive importance. It was only in the light of Sinai and the formation of God's people that questions of the ancestral past were raised: Where were we before Sinai and Egypt? The vivid accounts of the patriarchs—Abraham, Isaac, and Jacob—have all the color of family history; their significance is derived from what the descendants of these patriarchs came to be. That memory was extremely important. The personalities of the patriarchs are refracted through the prism of a people's experience, which saw the hand of God at work over a long and at times twisted history.

THE PAST

It should not surprise us that Yahweh's initial dealings with Abraham are described in covenant terms. The account in Genesis is preserved for us in both the Yahwist (J) and the priestly (P) traditions. While both accounts center on God's engagement in Abraham's life and the assurance of a favored future, they have very real differences.

Abram. In the Yahwist account (Gn 15) the aging Abram (whose name has not yet been changed) laments his childlessness and is given assurance of future progeny, even unlimited offspring (vv. 1–6). In addition, he is to inherit the land to which the guiding hand of God has led him (v. 7). This pledge is solemnized in the language of covenant binding God and Abram (v. 18). What is actually said is that they "cut a covenant" in an unusual ritual centering on the slaughter and splitting of a heifer, a goat, a ram, a dove, and a pigeon. A smoking brazier or censer then passed through the separated parts as the words of promise were heard by Abram. In the culture of the times the parties to an agreement would walk between severed animal parts to signify their willingness to share a similar fate if they failed to comply with the terms of the accord.

In the Yahwist account the covenant is predominantly unilateral. Nothing explicit is asked of Abram. The fiery pot symbolizes Yahweh pledging of himself to the agreement, but there is no similar action on the patriarch's part. Implicit, however, is Abram's continued willingness to comply with Yahweh's plan. What is highlighted is God's initiative in freely espousing the patriarch and his progeny.

In the priestly account of this promise (chap. 17) there is no mention of any ritual, although the assurance of offspring and land remains the same (vv. 3–8). In this version of the event, however, a promise is exacted from Abram. Every male descendant is to be circumcised (vv. 9–14). This was a practice not unknown to ancient cultures, but here it is given a religious significance as the sign of a covenanted people. Also, at this point Abram's name is changed to Abraham. What was originally nothing more than a difference in dialects is here explained (popularly) as meaning "father of a host of nations" (v. 5).

Both accounts of the Abrahamitic covenant are overlaid with the perspectives and practices of a later era, but it is the *berith* that is to the fore. By retrojection the event of the thirteenth century fleshes out an early memory six centuries removed. Viewed through the prism of Sinai, Yahweh's dealings with Abraham are seen to have a truly prophetic dimension; the bonding with a people was a story long in the making.[1]

Noah. Inevitably the next question arises: Where were we before Abraham? When speaking of the "twilight zone" of prehistory, we are obviously not speaking of historical recall. The importance of the first eleven chapters of Genesis lies in theological statement, not the recounting of events. It is the account of God's relationship to creation, with humanity standing at the pinnacle of consideration. Here human revolt comes to the fore as the struggle between the world of good and evil begins to emerge. It is within that context that the covenant with Noah speaks the language of divine engagement.

The ninth chapter of Genesis opens with a blessing that echoes the blessing presented at the time of the creation of man and woman (Gn 1:28). To Noah it is said, "Be fertile and multiply and fill the earth." What is missing, however, is that idyllic picture of peace and harmony among all creatures that was such an integral part of initial creation. Sin has already wreaked havoc. The early effects were present: a dry and unyielding soil for man to cultivate, pain in childbirth for the woman, and a groveling posture for the slithering snake (Gn 3:14–19). With human conduct becoming more sin-prone as Genesis unfolds, nature becomes equally distorted; misbegotten giants roam the earth and the threat of a massive flood appears on the horizon. In the wake of the deluge the animals, which Adam had earlier named (Gn 2:20), now flee in fear from the human predator (9:2).

Humans passing from a vegetarian to a carnivorous state (9:3) is seen as a concession to their weakened and sin-prone state. Killing and death are now part of the human experience (chap. 4), and the taking of animal life further seals this disintegration. Yet from God's side, in what will become eventually a biblical given, there is always the positive dimension, the new possibilities, the glass that is half full rather than half empty. Never again, God pledges, will there be a universal disaster or a cataclysmic upheaval, and a covenant will seal the promise (9:9ff.). While covenant terminology enhances the significance of the promise, it is a decision that is wholly unilateral. There is no human response to be elicited; divine initiative is to the fore. The absence of any human component is also occasioned by the fact that it is with the whole of creation that the *berith* is made.

But there is still the visible sign, the permanent reminder of a faithful God. The overarching rainbow readily conveys the idea of a juncture between heaven and earth, and this is precisely the function it serves in Genesis. With the retreat of the flood-waters, the rainbow emerges as the sign of peace and accord. It is the sign that tells the story, the myth that moves the soul, as is so often the case in biblical thought. The rainbow says it all. Chastisement is not forever; salvation will save the day.

Adam. We do not find the explicit language of covenant in the Genesis creation account, even though there are striking parallels between the Adam story and the covenants that are part of the biblical tradition. In the priestly tradition (Gn 1), with the completion of the six days of work Yahweh gifts the first couple with the goods of the earth and gives them dominion over all other creatures (Gn 1:28–29). This is the imagery of covenant, if nothing else. In the Yahwist narrative (chaps. 2–3) Adam is placed in a verdant garden wherein God's continued favor looks only for a response of obedience to a single precept: the couple is not to eat the fruit of a single tree (2:16f.). Again, this fits the covenant bilateral mold. With the "sin," the bonding relationship is ruptured and they are excluded from the garden.

With the idea of the pair being "placed" in the garden, a singular relationship between Yahweh and the pair is introduced in the narrative. It foreshadows a people taken from Egypt and constituted an elect group, the recipients of covenant and law, and, like Adam and Eve, distinctive in the whole order of creation. The single precept is paralleled in the dictates of divine will enshrined in the decalogue and covenant code. That grateful response, which undergirds biblical law, is foregone in Genesis in the interests of a sinful pursuit cunningly presented by a wily serpent. It is a transgression not unlike the desire for a "god who will be our leader" in the post-Sinai calf of gold incident (Ex 32:1–6). In short, the Genesis narrative gives us the leitmotif of covenant events to come.[2]

REMEMBERING...

Who has not been entranced as someone in touch with the family past recounts a story not heard before? There are the grandparents, the great aunts and uncles, whose foibles we are all too ready to overlook and whose accomplishments grow with the telling. Israel, too, had a family history, and that is what Genesis is about. But as we admire the obedience of Abraham, the skills of Jacob, and the obedience of Joseph, we know that this is much more than paging through a picture album of the past. The question was not solely Where were we before Sinai?, but

Where was God before Sinai? The answer is trumpeted in clarion tones, He was with us from the start. In guiding our forefathers, with their strengths and weaknesses, he was reaching out to all of us. In speaking of covenants with Abraham or Noah, the language itself is one of engagement. If there is any one message woven into the very fabric of the scriptures, it is that of God's involvement.

There is a theodicy that tells us that God was in no way obliged to become involved in his creation. Yet the language of scripture is an affair of the heart, the poetry of divine compulsion, as divine goodness focuses on a particular people in a clearly defined part of the world at a given moment in history. The early chapters of Genesis expand those horizons in highlighting a God related to all peoples, indeed to all creation. The language of covenant comes to the fore as a generous God continually shows favor to a people who, on the face of it, merit scant attention.

Covenant teaches us that people matter. The Noah covenant teaches us that all of creation matters. The Judeo-Christian tradition has never espoused a dualism between matter and spirit or a chasm separating God and the world. If the first chapter of Genesis teaches that what comes from God is good, then the Noah story indicates that human sinfulness will never succeed in severing the link between God and the universe that the rainbow so aptly depicts. It is small wonder that the New Testament hymns the sacredness of the cosmos, now touched by the redemptive blood of God's Son. For Paul, Christ is not only head of the church but the center of the whole of creation (Col 1; Eph 1).[3]

Considerations such as these are the theological underpinnings for environmental concern. Francis of Assisi was not a hopeless romantic; rather, he was fully aware of the language that creation speaks. If the world were seen as a sacrament of God's generosity and love, then we would scarcely be hurled toward the precipice of environmental ruin. Ecology is much more than a social concern; it is related to faith. None of us is exempt from the serious demands it makes.

The Future

Hope springs eternal in the human heart, or so says the poet. In the midst of incredible failure, setback, disintegration, even massive destruction, there is always the hope of a better day. In many instances that hope is actualized. In the words of hillside residents of a California town whose homes had been washed away by incessant heavy rain, "By this time next year we will have rebuilt." The human spirit is evidently indestructible. It displays formidable resilience. It hopes against hope.

Religion builds on that human quality. For much of Israel's history hope was centered on an earth-renewing kingdom of God. It had its "heavenly" dimension, but it was very much earth centered: a faithful kingship, a vast and peaceful kingdom, a God-fearing people. These were the limits imposed by a developing and evolving understanding of God and his relationship to the world. Yet belief in God's trustworthiness proved to be a strong motivating ethical force. The fact that the benefits of that hope may principally redound to the good of one's children or grandchildren did not diminish its force in guiding human conduct. As we shall see, that hope shaped the institution of prophetic utterance in Israel's post-Sinaitic history.

New Testament teaching does not prescind from hope in the earthly kingdom of God. But it is coupled with the belief in an eternal destiny. Jesus proclaimed a kingdom incipiently present in his own preaching but also a kingdom yet to come. The early church proclaims a Christ who is to return. Christian hope is anything but weak-kneed wishful thinking. Paul insists that the Spirit in whom we now stand is the pledge or first installment of eternal life. Our confidence is centered on the fact that Christ has already accomplished the major feat in bringing us from death to life in baptism; he will certainly go the "last mile" to bring us home.

Just as Israel looked to the past in the light of the covenant, it also looked to the future, and this, not only in terms of the land of peace and prosperity, but also of the permanent and lasting recognition of Yahweh's sovereignty. In the face of repeated failure, the hope endured—hope of a worthy Davidic descendant, a people responsive to covenant commitment, a country marked by peace and serenity. But it was Sinai that launched this hope. It now remains for us to look at the ways in which that hope was operative.

AFTER SINAI

The covenant gave meaning to Israelite life during the centuries that followed Sinai. Even when the language of covenant was not particularly prominent, as in the case of some of the early prophets, there is no doubt that it served as a constant backdrop to ethical and theological discourse within the Hebrew community throughout its history. There are accounts of covenant renewal, such as that conducted by Joshua after the occupation (Jos 24) and in the time of Ezra after the exile (Neh 9–10). Moreover, many of the psalms reflect strong covenant strains in their composition. Two major moments in any study of the *berith* are the covenant with David (2 Sm 7) and the pledge of a future bond in Jeremiah (Jer 31).

Covenant Renewal. The ceremony conducted at Shechem in Joshua's time represents something of a bridge in the Deuteronomic history. In Israelite history there were ceremonies in which the reading of the law figured prominently; there are fewer instances of an actual rite of covenant renewal. The ceremony at Shechem celebrates the successful occupation of the land as promised by Yahweh, a moment in which the people commit themselves anew to their Sinai promises.

But the scenario as presented in Joshua 24 is not without its difficulties. There is not a shred of biblical or archeological evidence for any destruction or upheaval at Shechem when the Hebrews invaded Palestine; it is not mentioned as one of the pillaged cities; and, in fact, what extra-biblical information there is points to its uninterrupted habitation in the twelfth and thirteenth centuries B.C.[4] Therefore what is presented as a renewal ceremony may well have been a rite of inclusion incorporating already present Canaanites into the covenant community. These would have been people who had never participated in the Exodus event and thus, in reading between the lines it may be possible to see both covenant renewal and covenant making. It comes at a moment at the end of the book of Joshua, wherein the land of promise has been bestowed and the beginning of a hope filled future dawns.

This is also a moment of consolidation for the Israelite tribes. There is much that is left unsaid in the biblical narratives about skirmishes and battles, the displacement of people, and the incorporation of disparate groups about which we can only speculate. What is presented as a neat parceling out of the country among the twelve descendants of Jacob was—and about this there is little doubt—historically a quite different matter. Much of this grouping of people along "tribal" lines is artificial. The invading Israelite population together with people of very disparate and heterogeneous backgrounds began a process of cultural and religious assimilation resulting in what might be termed a federation of states, each identified with one of the sons of Jacob. This protracted development is capsulized in the ceremony recorded in Joshua 24.[5]

Even the account of the Shechem renewal had an extended history before its final Deuteronomic editing. Its basic features reflect a long and familiar history of covenant making. There is the historical recall of God's saving action in the past (vv. 2–13), a summons to the people to reject all other deities, with a concomitant willingness to accept the covenant terms (vv. 14–24), followed by the erection of the memorial stone (vv. 26f.). The emphasis on Yahweh's broad sovereignty over the nations, reflected in Israel's pagan ancestry (v. 2), events of the Egyptian sojourn (vv. 4ff.), and the overthrow of the Amorites (vv. 8ff.) fits well with the thesis that the ceremony was originally designed to incorporate non-Hebrew peoples.

Of note is the fact that the litany of God's saving action is quite selective, looking exclusively to the Hebrews' dealings with foreign powers, with no mention made of the Sinai covenant or the desert sojourn. The strong emphasis placed on the call to fidelity and the rejection of false gods (vv. 14–24) seems almost oblivious of Israel's past commitment to do precisely that (Ex 20:2–4). All of this makes considerable sense, however, if "new covenanters" are being incorporated into a monotheistic faith. In true covenant form, however, the plea for an exclusive acceptance of Yahweh is based on the favors received at the time of the Exodus.

There are no fewer than four positive responses from the people, reflecting, evidently, the chapter's liturgical setting during its lengthy history. With acceptance in place, the memorial stone witnesses to the moral solidarity of the people in making their commitment and is a lasting reminder of their pledge and the loss inherent in any eventual betrayal.

David. The extraordinary promise made to David by Yahweh through the prophet Nathan (2 Sm 7) is never referred to as a covenant in its original context but is so designated elsewhere (Ps 89:4). In the original oracle there is the dominant note of Yahweh's pledge to David and his posterity. While the agreement is heavily weighted on the side of God's initiative, it does call for a just moral posture on the part of future kings (2 Sm 7:14).[6]

The transition from the period of tribal federation to that of the monarchy, as reflected in the books of Joshua and Judges, was evidently not an easy one. There was tension over the idea of any king replacing Yahweh's sovereignty, or even competing with it, and this is clearly reflected in the biblical text. It is not difficult to find strong anti-monarchical sentiments (1 Sm 8) as well as equally strong pro-monarchical feeling (1 Sm 9–10). Discussion centers around the origin of these distinctly opposite views, for example, separate traditions, Deuteronomic editing, and so forth. What seems certain is that the negative description of what kingship would inevitably bring (1 Sm 8:1–10) is clearly based on the lived experience of the excesses of the Solomonic and post-Solomonic era.

The Kingship and Yahweh's Sovereignty. Whatever may be said of the political implications of the monarchy, the major problem centered on its infringement on the exclusive sovereignty of Yahweh. The Sinai covenant had established such close ties between the people and their God that the insertion of any type of human leader into the equation created insurmountable difficulties in many quarters. Regardless of how the designation and reign of Saul actually came about, in its literary presentation the Deuteronomist sees it as a compromise at best. That the royal establishment won acceptance in time and even became the conduit of a future messianic hope cannot conceal its controversial origins.

The context of 2 Samuel 7, wherein the covenant with David is established, has its own literary complexity. It gives evidence of having been reworked and edited over a considerable period of time. Its importance resides in the fact that it launches Israel's centuries-long belief in the lasting character of the Davidic line, which pointed to a definitive reign of peace and justice presided over by a descendant of David. As the chapter opens, David is disturbed by the fact that, while he lives in royal luxury, the Lord lacks a permanent dwelling, there being only the tent that housed the ark of the covenant. David is determined to correct this situation and is encouraged in his resolve by the trusted prophet Nathan. In a throwback to a previous era of greater simplicity, Yahweh declines the offer in favor of the freedom and mobility the ark life offers, a relic of a more idyllic pre-monarchical period. In reading between the lines one cannot escape the political ambitions in David's desire to see a temple constructed in Jerusalem. Doing so would solidify his own royal authority by making Jerusalem the center of cultic and political life (vv. 1–7).

Yahweh's response shows as much concern for the people as it does for David (vv. 8–11). True, David's fortune will reflect Yahweh's continued support in the future no less than in the past, but the Lord also desires to see the people firmly settled in the land and free from the incursions of hostile forces. So it is God who will build a "house" for David, not vice versa (v. 11b), in a characteristic play on words. David was envisioning a temple as a house for the Lord, whereas Yahweh clearly refers to the "house of David" as a dynasty. Up to this point the prophecy is generic, a reference to God's continued presence with the line of David; however, there is then a reference to a house to be erected by a specific son of David, a clear reference to Solomon's temple (v. 13). This is a literary insert, intrusive to the text, introduced at some later point in recognition of the temple's construction by David's son.

Reconciling Two Covenants. How, then, does this covenant with David fit into the larger picture of the Sinai covenant? The answer is best found in the scene of David's final conversation with Solomon before the former's death (1 Kgs 2–4). The

Deuteronomic exhortation to all the people "to keep the commandments of the LORD, your God, and the ordinances and statutes he has enjoined on you" sees in the country's king the primary one in whom these values are to be invested. Those who rule in the line of David are to be found faithful "with their whole heart and their whole soul." Only then are they assured Yahweh's continued support in upholding the Davidic kingship. It should be noted that here in the book of Kings text this promise of support is more conditioned than that found in 2 Samuel 7, where it is seen as irrevocable. The portrait of the ideal king painted in Deuteronomy (17:14–20) presents him as a true covenant observer, modest in his selection of both wives and horses, an assiduous student and observer of Torah, and a man close to his people. In short, in his life and example the king is to be the first supporter of the Sinai covenant.

The fact that most of the kings of Judah and Israel failed miserably as role models of covenant fidelity made of the Deuteronomic teaching a hope that overreached reality. But the principle remained the same. The king stood within and not above the covenant; only in this way could the monarchy be given theological justification. What makes the later King Josiah a model of Yahwistic faith is the fact that upon finding the "book of the law" in the temple, he committed himself to a reform wholly centered in its statutes and decrees (2 Kgs 22–23). It was a covenant-centered reign, while the waywardness and defiance of other kings put them beyond the pale of covenant fidelity; they are summarily dismissed as having done "evil in the sight of the LORD."

THE HUMAN MIX

The monarchy was a very mixed blessing, and therein lies the paradox. It was born of mixed feelings, of pros and cons, of negative and positive reactions. Aa far as Judah was concerned, at its best the monarchy produced David, Hezekiah, and Josiah. One would like to include Solomon on that list, but that largely depends on which chapter of 1 Kings is being read. On the positive side, adjustment to the monarchy brought with it hopes for a better future and closer adherence to Yahweh's will in a messianic era. On the negative side, it brought a type of corrupt leadership as distant from true Yahwism as the conduct of any non-believing monarch. The prophets inveighed against kings and priests, "the crown and the cross."

Religion would be so much different if we were not so human. But the fact is that we are not disembodied spirits; we are not gnostics or adherents of celestial "mystery religions." Everything about the Judeo-Christian tradition is incarnational, from the "enlivened flesh" of Genesis 1–2 to the Word who "became flesh" of John 1. The scriptures, the church, the sacraments, the hierarchy—all are grace in fragile vessels. So it was, and so it will always be.

In this state of redemption we remain between the "now" and the "not yet"; flesh and spirit still struggle within us. What ultimately counts is the triumph of the spirit; that which is purely human has to be discounted. Kings with all their appurtenances had feet of clay, and those anti-monarchical strains conveyed the danger of substituting king for God. The danger of an organized church in which the Spirit blows where and as he wills is that we become overly fixed on what is human and passing away, all that which is of no consequence

We become torn apart over issues, polarized over ideologies. Often we become centered around our human heroes, our Kephas, our Paul, our Apollo. Yet we hardly hear the words of the Apostle: "Was Paul crucified for you?" The human dimension of the church is truly integral, but unless it points beyond itself, we are hopelessly lost. Everything that the church does and is must converge on Christ, who in turn is the window on God. Only when the first truly realize that they must be last, when the leaders of the church grasp the truth that they cannot resemble the kings and rulers of this world, and when all of us act as if Christ alone matters will the message of the gospels ring true.

RECOMMITMENT

How true it is that all of us stand under the judgment of the Word. Scripture is the criterion on which theology rests. Every statement of the magisterium must reflect the Word of God; our ethic must be rooted there as well. The same is true of everything that makes church to be what it is. When the Jesus of the sermon on the mount excludes oath-taking in the Christian community on the basis that honesty in word should make it absolutely superfluous, indeed demeaning, and the church repeatedly asks people, even those in sacred office, to take oaths, there is something seriously amiss. It is at best an admission that Christians are nowhere near where they should be.

At Shechem the Hebrews repeated their commitment—as we do every time we make the act of contrition or renew our baptismal promises. Every Holy Thursday priests in the church recommit themselves to their ordination promises. And how many times have we been invited to the twenty-fifth or fiftieth wedding anniversary of couples who wish to say yes to one another once again. Even more than the initial engagement, this is a moment of solidarity and congratulations. In Israel these were the moments when later generations affirmed once again the commitment of their forebears. Doing so is no less important today. Yes, we can go on forever saying "I believe" or "I do," but to solemnize our commitment liturgically says it in a public and sacred forum, which gives new meaning to the whole reality. We all need symbols, signs, and rituals, and life is full of them. Milestones are all marked: first communion, confirmation, graduation, marriage, ordination; the preparations never seem to end. And the afterglow means smiling faces, which speak volumes on the meaning of life.

Yet we must also celebrate accomplishment, and that means not only recognition but encouragement. When Israelites renewed the covenant, they looked to the past as well as the future. And so do we. Every mass in which we participate renews the covenant once again, as we give our yes to God. Every time we celebrate the sacrament of reconciliation, sorrow and a purpose of amendment come to the fore. We cannot live without these benchmarks. They are concrete, visible reminders of our humanness and of God's goodness. These are God-centered moments in life in which gratitude, contrition, thanks, and petition play a prominent part. As often as we may wish for those silent moments of interior reflection, we can never divorce ourselves spiritually or psychologically from that sense of community, of group affirmation and support, which is at the heart of what Israel did and what the church has done for centuries. As much as we may wish it otherwise, we are never alone. We are part of a common journey. Sinai and Shechem come to life again in every parish mass or community celebration of eucharist. The history of our tradition is not simply there for scholars searching through dusty volumes. It is not antiquated and lifeless, a worthwhile pursuit for those who know Hebrew and Greek. It is alive and vibrant and touches what we do day after day and week after week. Every time we as community say our yes to God it is covenant renewal once again.

A FUTURE COVENANT

The period of the Babylonian exile, which spanned a large part of the sixth century B.C., can best be described as a time of political defeat and national humiliation. The northern kingdom had been earlier overthrown; Judah and Jerusalem lay in ruins after the incursion of the Babylonians under Nebuchadnezzar and the deportation of a large part of the population. From a purely human point of view the future looked very bleak indeed. Ironically, however, the prophetic literature flourished during this period in the work of Jeremiah, Ezekiel, and second Isaiah. With the loss of its central institutions, not to speak of the land of promise itself, Israel moved closer to the heart of its faith in a deeper awareness of its relationship with God. It was in this context that hopes for the future centered on a new and permanent covenant of the heart.

While this promise appears in Ezekiel (37:26), it is Jeremiah who spells out most clearly its essential features (31:31–34). The context in which it appears speaks of the liberation of the deported people and their return from the oppression of exile; it does this in a series of four poems, each of which expresses the hopes accompanying restoration. The first poem (vv. 1–6) betrays a distinctly northern provenance, with its references to Israel, Samaria, and Mount Ephraim. Assyria ceased to be a power with its defeat in 612, giving rise to a strong belief in the return of the Israelite deportees captured at the time of Assyria's

48

conquest of the north. Thus the poem stems from this earlier moment in the career of Jeremiah, even though its present context finds it in a chapter dealing with all the deportees, especially those taken by the Babylonians.

The First Hymn. Covenant language appears early in the first hymn in underscoring the God-people relationship (v. 1) and a covenant love *(hesed)* that has never ceased (v. 3). It is a picture of merrymaking and festivity that sees the people once again drawing on the riches of their native soil. The separation of north from south, of Samaritan from Jerusalem worship, will be overcome as a newly reunited people of Yahweh sees Mount Zion and Jerusalem as its point of convergence (v. 6).

The Second Hymn. In this hymn (vv. 7–14) the glories of the return are sung as the people make their way home from distant lands, in language and imagery reminiscent of second Isaiah (chaps. 40 and 43). It is the *remnant* of Israel that is saved (v. 7). All too often the sin of God's people has been in tension with the Lord's plan of salvation, yet there was always the belief that God's fidelity required that at least a segment of the population be preserved from disaster. In time, the emphasis shifted to the spiritual characteristics of the remnant, embodying those features of covenant faithfulness from the human side befitting salvation. Here once again it is the less fortunate who make the journey home, the poor of God *(anawim)* so visible in the blind, the lame, and the expectant mother (v. 8; Is 35:5f.). Just as in the case of the remnant, the "poor of God" gradually move from a social category of dependence on God and society to one that pointed up the interior qualities characterizing a truly spiritual dependence.

As the journey is made on a road that has been made level near providential waters that slake the desert thirst, the return becomes a witness to all peoples of God's redeeming love (vv. 9–11). This note of universalism is repeatedly struck in the prophets: the nations are "evangelized" not through preaching and proclamation but by witnessing the power and love of Yahweh at work among his people (Is 42:10–18; 43:9f.). Material blessings at their best await the returning remnant: grain, wine, oil, abundant water, and festivities, while traditional terms of endearment link Yahweh and his people: father, shepherd, and redeemer (vv. 9–13).

The Third Hymn (vv. 15–20). The matriarchal figure Rachel, the mother of Joseph and grandmother of Ephraim and Manasseh (Gn 46:20), was closely linked with the northern kingdom. Her burial place at Ramah, a few miles north of Jerusalem (1 Sm 10:2), is to the fore in the third hymn of the chapter, as she mourns the northern deportees. She is consoled by the promise of their return (vv. 16f.). In the plea of Ephraim (the northern kingdom), which follows (vv. 18f.), the nuances of "return" have singular importance in pointing up the theological dimension given a word's original meaning. We have seen it already in the question of "the poor" and "the remnant"; here it appears in the Hebrew verb *shub,* meaning basically a turn on the road or more precisely "a turning back." From there it was but a step to its use in the sense of moral conversion, that is, a turning one's life around. When Ephraim says (in a literal sense): "If you allow me, I will return" (v. 18b), the physical journey embraces the more important change of moral direction. The language of the context is clearly that of repentance and conversion.

The Final Hymn. Here attention turns to the highway, as the fickle "virgin" Israel is called to return in what is both a geographical and moral journey (vv. 21–23). A strong appeal is made for her to end her waywardness with the dawn of a new era of fidelity wherein the woman (Israel) will totally envelop the man (Yahweh), in a way quite contrary to the spiritual vagaries of her past married life. An oracle pledges future blessings for the south, that is, Judah and the capital Jerusalem (vv. 23–26). This clearly situates the final oracle during the Babylonian deportation, sometime after 586. In words that speak of restoration, a time of building and planting after the ordeal of destruction and demolition that echo the prophet's commission (1:10), it serves as an appropriate introduction to the promise of the new covenant, the climactic passage of the chapter.

THE PROMISE OF A NEW COVENANT

A word of background to this singular oracle. The Hebrews' sense of solidarity made them exponents of the notion of collective guilt, together with their neighbors in the Near Eastern world. Just as the action of one could bring blessings upon many, misconduct also cast a wide net. Sons paid for the sins of their fathers (Ex 20:5); the entire household of the Egyptian pharaoh suffered for the ruler's sin against Abraham (Gn 12:17); their families paid a costly price for the sin of Dathan and Abiram (Nm 16:31f.). In the present oracle Jeremiah indicates that such will not be the case in the future; each person and that person alone will be responsible for his or her personal conduct (Jer 31:29f.). In rejecting a maxim that evidently had common coinage at the time, envisioning the children gritting their teeth over the bitter grapes their elders had eaten (Ez 18:2), the prophet makes a strong point of the personal relationship with God that stands at the heart of religious experience. Sanction for sin will be visited upon its perpetrator, and there it will rest.

This is not to say that a sense of solidarity is lost, and that everything is reduced to religious personalism. There is still the realization that salvation (however it is described) comes to the individual as member of a larger body. Israel's sense of community was deeply imbedded in the national psyche. It was a part of Yahwistic faith and was to carry into the New Testament as well. In fact, it was this notion of extended culpability that had given some leverage to the whole question of sanctions. Since sin had to be dealt with in the present life and not beyond the grave, it gave some measure of solace to the innocent sufferer to see his pain as inherited from earlier perpetrators. However, with the exile and the accompanying demise of many institutions and traditional tenets, it is one's personal responsibility for good or evil conduct that plays center stage. It serves as a very apt introduction to the following verses, which speak of the covenant to come.

This promise of a future bond with God (Jer 31:31–34) is a high point in Old Testament thought. First of all, it should be seen as in basic continuity with Israel's past and not as a rupture in the God-people relationship. It is made with Israel and Judah and has the same binding effect on both parties as did the former covenant. There is no new body of laws to be conferred. All the component elements of the former bond are presumed to be present. The difference lies in the way in which it will be actualized.

What the former covenant was in theory, the new will become

in practice. Where the former was repeatedly violated, the new will be marked by observance (v. 32). Like the aforementioned principle of retribution, this covenant is profoundly personal and internalized, with the law written "upon their hearts" (v. 33). No longer cast in stone, this is a law deeply understood and willed, a covenant law that will be owned. The mediation of teachers and interpreters will be unnecessary as God communicates directly with the believer. In language admittedly figurative, a new reality is nevertheless unveiled. Within the broader community context, the love of God touches the individual in a way that is personal and experiential. The response from the heart to a sovereign divine will springs from sentiments that bespeak a "knowledge of God" that goes beyond the cerebral and envelops the entire person.

This is not an anti-institutional prophecy, although it comes from a period in history when structured life in Israel was minimal. But the experience of exile, with its dismembering of institutions, paved the way for this deeper sense of religion envisioned by the prophet. Traditional institutions may not be ruled out, but they are relativized. The emphasis is not on the law but the spirit in which it is lived. From their vantage point, Christians see in this doctrinal development pointers toward the life in God to be initiated with the death and resurrection of Jesus.[7]

EQUAL AND HOLY BEFORE GOD

To see the immensely positive side of covenant is not to ignore its inherent dangers. God could easily be dealt with as a partner to an agreement and therefore bound to it under any circumstances. In subtle ways it could leave God open to "manipulation" in ways never originally envisioned. The suggestion has been made that this was one of the reasons why some of the earlier prophets, while never unmindful of the covenant, rather studiously avoided the term. Their writings often indicate an atmosphere of proud self-assurance among the Hebrews of the time. Also, one can see how the covenant with David led to a certain overconfidence in viewing Yahweh as the guarantor of the Davidic line. It is safe to say that dangers of this kind were unavoidable.

Other ideas flow from our considerations of the covenant at this moment in its evolution. There were certainly struggles and sharply opposing views on the implications of the Davidic covenant; it could not become a contender with the broader bond between Yahweh and his people. In a very real sense the Sinai covenant was the great equalizer. God's outreach to his people left no room for rank or privilege, a point that will become even clearer with the emergence of the New Testament covenant. Religion has never succeeded in avoiding the trappings of institutionalism and probably never will. Structures are inevitable in any organization. As soon as a newly formed club decides it will meet on Wednesdays, it is already structured. The monarchy within Israel certainly did not escape these pitfalls. The kings looked very much like their counterparts on the world stage and even in their conduct were all too often indistinguishable. In a religious society anyone invested with authority must constantly reflect on his or her relationship to the entire community. This is particularly true in the Judeo-Christian tradition. All authority must see itself in relation to the people that is loved and saved. While the Hebrews were granted a king, his position was one of subordination to the law as in the case of any other Israelite. In terms of observance he was to be an example to his people.

The new covenant of Jeremiah triggers myriad reflections. First and foremost, there is the interiority of religious faith. Observance has its own importance, but unless it flows from a deep, personal relationship with God, it becomes mere formalism. God is often seen as appeased or mollified by observance, and one's personal interests are somehow safeguarded. "Each morning bring your sacrifices, every third day your tithes; burn leavened food as a thanksgiving sacrifice, proclaim publicly your freewill offerings. For so you love to do, O men of Israel, says the Lord GOD" (Am 4:4f.). It becomes so easy to forget that religion is basically a matter of the heart. Only when God has been allowed to touch us in a personal and internal way does observance become a loving and gracious response. The fact that the percentage of Catholics attending mass is reasonably high gives us scant consolation, especially if Christian comportment is scarcely distinguishable from that of society as a whole. Faith is called to make a difference, and it will do so only to the extent that it truly fashions conduct. That happens when it comes from within, from the realization that because God has touched us nothing will ever be quite the same again.

God of the covenant, at so many stages in our religious history you have been present to your people, always with love and concern. We cannot believe that it is any different now, especially at a time when our needs are so great. Give us the grace to see your hand in the events that surround us. In a very confused and confusing world, guide us in the way of your covenant on the path that leads to life eternal. Amen.

FOR STUDY AND DISCUSSION

1. Can we speak of tradition as our religious memory?
2. There is a link between the Sinai covenant and the earlier patriarchs, whose memory is evoked by this bond with God. Explain the connection.
3. Were the earlier covenants (Abram, Noah) seen as bilateral or unilateral? What is the significance for today of the covenant with Noah embracing the universe?
4. Do you see covenant motifs in the Adam and Eve story?
5. Discuss the traditional covenant features in Joshua's renewal at Shechem (Jos 24).
6. When do we, as Christians, experience covenant renewal?
7. In light of the Sinai covenant, what difficulties were present in the covenant with David?
8. What were the historical circumstances surrounding the events described in Jeremiah 31?
9. How does the new covenant of Jeremiah 31 differ from its predecessor?
10. The covenant highlights the equality of all covenanters. What are some of the implications of this for the church today?

4

THE COVENANT IN CHRIST

*"You have approached...Jesus, the mediator of a new covenant, and the
sprinkled blood that speaks more eloquently than that of Abel."*
(Heb 12:22–24)

The Sinai covenant was the focal point of Israelite history, with
both subsequent and previous events refracted through its
prism. The covenant has left its imprint on the whole of the Old
Testament. The new covenant that Jesus inaugurates plays a similar role in the New Testament. It is the death-resurrection of
Christ that opens the era of the new covenant, marked by the
presence of the Spirit, and serves as the prism through which the
entire ministry of Jesus is viewed. For example, when Jesus
announces the time of fulfillment, the arrival of the kingdom of
God and the gospel at the beginning of his Galilean ministry, the
full understanding of what that means in terms of the resurrection is present to the evangelist.

It is in the setting of the Last Supper that the new covenant
emerges with the greatest clarity. It is there that Matthew, Mark,
and Luke place the institution of the eucharist, most appropriately, since in the life of the early church it was the eucharist that
reaffirmed and perpetuated the new alliance between God and
his people.[1]

The Passover Question. In all three synoptic accounts the Last
Supper coincides with the annual celebration of the Jewish
Passover (Mk 14:12–16; Mt 26:17–19; Lk 22:7–13), and in this
they are at odds with John, for whom this is a significant farewell
supper, with no mention of either Passover or eucharist. There
are theological reasons for this divergence on both sides. The
synoptics place Passover that year on Thursday-Friday (evening

to evening), while John places it on Friday-Saturday, making of that sabbath "a great sabbath." This becomes clear when the Jews in the fourth gospel do not want to enter Pilate's praetorium, because such defilement would make it impossible for them to eat the Passover that evening (18:28). Moreover, Jesus is sentenced on the "preparation day for Passover" (19:14), with his death on Friday coinciding with the traditional slaying of the lambs for the feast.

It is clear that both the synoptics and John had their reasons for placing Passover where they did. The synoptic tradition wanted to telescope the eucharist and the death of Jesus, since it is the latter event that gives meaning to the former; thus simple logic meant keeping them as close together as possible. Moreover, the eucharist unfolds against the background of the Passover, the major feast of Hebrew deliverance and salvation. Therefore, regardless of the original historical circumstances of eucharistic institution (and it belongs to the earliest layer of Christian tradition), other factors touching on the significance of the institution come to the fore. By the same token, John is interested in drawing the death of Jesus as close to Passover as possible, again with the redemptive motif placed in strong relief. It is for these reasons that it is so difficult to determine which tradition stands closer to the historical fact, since this was not the dominant concern of any of the evangelists.

The chronology of the events of Christ's final days as given in John has logic in its favor. A farewell supper with his disciples, followed by his arrest and rapid sentencing, would have Jesus' execution take place before the "great sabbath" on which Passover was to be celebrated that year. Thus, Jesus is removed from the cross in order that the feast not be profaned (Jn 19:31). This means, of course, that it makes it impossible for us to determine when the eucharist was instituted, since the synoptics' dating becomes wholly theological. What cannot be gainsaid, however, is the antiquity of the eucharist in the life of the church. In the early fifties Paul speaks of its already being firmly fixed in liturgical tradition, already centering on the night before Christ's death (1 Cor 11:23–26). From the historical evidence alone this points strongly to the eucharist's derivation from

Christ, even if the actual historical circumstances cannot be pinpointed with certainty.

The Institution Accounts. The farewell supper in John is the scene of one of Jesus' most prolonged discourses (chaps. 14–17). In the synoptics it is truncated and focuses principally on the eucharist (Mt 26:26–29; Mk 14:22–25; Lk 22:15–20). Moreover, the highly stylized account of the institution and its unrelatedness to the Passover ritual points to its insertion in the narrative and its origins in the liturgical life of the church. If this were an actual Passover, it would be difficult to determine from the text at what point the eucharist occurred; only Luke makes mention of a cup "after they had eaten" (v. 20), or the third cup of the Passover meal. While in synoptic studies there is general agreement on the dependence of Matthew and Luke on the earlier Mark, the accounts of the institution reflect some interesting variants across the board. Mark and Matthew have strong similarities in the eucharistic formula, while Luke is closer to Paul's account (1 Cor 11:23–26). It has been suggested that we are faced with two distinct liturgical origins, that of Jerusalem (Matthew-Mark) and Antioch (Luke-Paul). Even within these traditions there are slight variations: Matthew's "take...*eat*" over Mark's "take"; Luke's "which will be shed for you" over the cup, absent in Paul; and the rubrical *anamnesis* "Do this in remembrance of me," found solely in the Luke-Paul tradition.

The *new* covenant is mentioned explicitly in both Luke and Paul, remaining implicit in the parallel tradition. The latter's "This is the blood of the covenant" is closer to the language of Moses in sealing the Sinai alliance (Ex 24:8). As in Exodus, sacrifice accompanied the covenant (Ex 24:5), so too the eucharistic symbolism and language are strongly sacrificial. The broken bread, the red wine, the Passover setting, the personal abstinence of Jesus at the table in connection with his being victim— all are symbolically related to the note of oblation. There is the blood "shed" and the body "given," with Matthew's explicit motivation: "for the forgiveness of sins." The meal setting of the eucharist evokes the reference to eating and drinking after the Sinai covenant (Ex 24:11).

Although brief and stylized in its synoptic presentation, the institution narrative is rich in its allusions embracing the Sinai covenant, Passover, and sacrifice in general.

As has been noted, the words of Jesus over the cup are a distinct echo of Moses' words at the conclusion of the covenant ritual. Yet Jesus' qualifying "my" is important. It is the new covenant that is inaugurated, the one spoken of by Jeremiah (31:31–34). This will be brought about by Christ's death-resurrection with its concomitant outpouring of the Spirit, who will pen that law written, not on stone tablets, but on the heart. The full implementation of the reign of God, which Jesus had preached, will then be definitively established. In strict continuity with covenant tradition, this is to be a binding relationship between Yahweh and his people, and yet its internal character will be strongly highlighted, and this for two reasons. The sacrificial death is not that of animal victims but of God's own son, who hands himself over in love. In addition, the Spirit is a sharing in God's own life, which ushers one into the household of God and enables the believer to address God in familiar terms as "Abba," Father (Rom 8:15). No other form of mediation is henceforth required; there is no need to single out "Master," "Rabbi," or "Father" (Mt 23:7–11). It is the Spirit who will inspire, educate, and guide. In this new covenant Christ is both priest and victim; God remains the initiator and divine partner, while the human component is variously designated as disciples, "men or women who belonged to the Way" (Acts 9:3), or simply "church" (Mt 16:18; 18:17).

Eucharist and Passover. Although the institution of the eucharist is shaped by clear Christian liturgical concerns, in the gospel narrative it is cast in the broader context of the Passover celebration. This major Jewish celebration recalls Yahweh's great act of deliverance from Egyptian tyranny, an event which reached its apogee in the Sinai covenant. The lamb recalls the moment of liberation when its blood was sprinkled on the doorposts, thus turning away the hand of the avenging spirit. The bitter herbs speak of the anguish of slavery and oppression; the unleavened bread, the rapidity of the departure from Egypt. At this Passover Christ acts as the head of the family. To the traditional question "What does this rite mean?" he would answer:

"This is the Passover sacrifice of the LORD" (Ex 12:27). All of this remains true in a Christian sense, even though it has now been transposed to a new key. Christ is now the paschal lamb by the shedding of whose blood we are delivered from the Egypt of sinful bondage and become party to a new covenant of the Spirit written on the heart.

Eucharist and the Servant Theme. Other features emerge in addition to this Passover-covenant theme. In an atonement that is vicarious and expiatory, Jesus is seen as the Isaian servant of the Lord (Is 52:3ff.). Identification of this figure who appears so strikingly and yet so elusively in the pages of Isaiah has always been difficult and has escaped any real consensus. At the same time, it is clear that the New Testament sees the role of Jesus in God's salvific plan against the background of the servant. In the eucharistic formula itself, this is the body and blood "given for you," "shed for many," "for the forgiveness of sins." Christ is the prototype of willing suffering on behalf of others, as the eucharistic narrative amply illustrates.

The Eucharist as Meal. The theme of the repast, connected with both Passover and Sinai (Ex 24:11), throws into relief the ancients' belief in the sacredness of meal sharing. This was to become one with the life and sentiments of another. To share food was to wish another well in a significant way; it brought strength and nourishment for life's journey (Gn 18:1–15). To share food with an enemy was to make a lie of the symbol. To eat a sacrificial victim was a form of communion with the deity, a view shared by adherents of other religions as well (1 Cor 8). In the eucharist this is more than a symbolic life sharing, with the clear identification of the sacrificial victim: *my* body, *my* blood. This sacramental realism surpasses the former linking of event and memorial of the Passover celebration.

And the eucharist is to be perpetuated. The rubric states it simply: "Do this in my *anamnesis.*" In fact, as we have seen, it is the liturgical life of the church, decades removed from the time of Christ, that provides the evangelists with the institution account. Each celebration is a living link with that saving event, resulting in the Christian's direct engagement in the paschal mystery. There will never be another death or another sacrifice;

nothing can add to the efficacy of what Christ has done once and for all. And yet it is made new and brought to life in every age and time. This is the meaning of sacrament.[2]

THE LIVED EXPERIENCE

It is called the new covenant; it forms a new people in a new Spirit. As long as there is word and sacrament it will never lose its newness. It is rather mind-boggling to think that what occurs daily in our parish church links us to the Jerusalem community of two thousand years ago. Liturgy requires a personal invest-ment, but it is never a personal act. The public character of wor-ship is evidenced in the established norms that surround its celebration, although these at times can become excessive and destructive of creativity. While excesses are always regrettable, the fact remains that cult is public and belongs to a public and sacred domain. The mass is the most sacred act of Christianity; it must of necessity be safeguarded. The mass draws us into contact with all that Christ accomplished in his own transition from flesh to glory and relates us to an even more ancient past, that of Passover, Sinai, and covenant. All of this is part of our sacred her-itage, not a musty and time worn legacy but one experienced anew with every celebration.

Eucharist and Church. In First Corinthians (10:14–17) Paul speaks of the two bodies: the body of Christ in the form of bread, and the body that is church. It is in sharing the one eucharistic bread that we, though many, become ever more the one ecclesial body. Today's emphasis on Christian community is annoying to some. It is said to be easier and more conducive to recollection to pray alone. So it may be. Yet in engaging himself in the mire of humanity, God accepted the consequences. The covenant did not always show the best side of the Israelites, nor does the new covenant always present Christians in the best possible light. But that is what life is all about: the light and shadows, the good news and the bad news. Christian community means saints and sinners, rich and poor, ethnic variations. There is a broad spectrum of thought and ideology, just as is found in the world at large. There are many variations in the way liturgy is offered in our churches from week to week. Mass may be inspiring or distracting; preaching may be enlightened or inadequate. This is what covenant is all about—the mix of life, the light and the shadow. Yet there is one message that reaches all of us. We are very much loved. Any move forward from whatever point begins on that note.

THE OLD AND THE NEW

If we concede that the new covenant supersedes the old and yet flows from it and builds upon it, it is legitimate to ask how much of the former dispensation becomes part of the new. More precisely, what is to become of Torah, the body of laws found in the Pentateuch, which fashioned every feature of Hebrew life? When Jeremiah spoke of the new covenant (31:31–34), he did not speak of new law or a termination of the old. Rather, he spoke of a new spirit that was to actualize the law. It should then come as no surprise that the question of the role of Torah was a major one in the life of the primitive church, and it was not easily resolved.

The Assembly of Jerusalem. The fifteenth chapter of the Acts of the Apostles presents a major assembly of church leaders in Jerusalem to decide the issue of the continuing validity of the Mosaic law for Gentile converts. This is a more prominent and noteworthy forum in the Lucan setting than the simpler account given by Paul in Galatians (2:1–10), even though the results are basically the same. The central question was whether or not those entering the church who had never known the law of Moses were to be held to its demands. In the face of what must have been considerable opposition, especially from members of the Jerusalem community, Paul argues forcefully against such a requirement, with a final accord reached with the Jerusalem authorities that, with the exception of some few precepts (Acts 15:29), the law was not to be binding on Gentile converts. The dispensation, however, did not extend to Jewish converts, for whom the law was evidently still in force. This diversity of outlook between the two major groups within the first-century church illustrates with striking clarity the struggle that was present in delineating the effects of the new covenant.[3]

PAUL AND THE LAW

For Paul, it was not simply a matter of not mixing the old and the new, of putting the new patch on the old garment, or new wine into an old wineskin. It was a question of the all-encompassing and exclusive means of salvation through Christ and Christ alone. Faith in Christ, and that alone, justifies us before God; to add any complementary requirement is nothing short of blasphemous. The noteworthy summary of Paul's position is found in his letter to the Romans (chaps. 5–7). He begins by lining up his forces on two opposing sides, one headed by Adam, the other by Christ. The parallel ends by highlighting the overriding benefits derived from Christ.

Romans 5. Paul begins by striking a dominant note of hope for the future centered on what Christ has already accomplished on our behalf (5:6–11). He presents his case in this way: In what would be termed a truly heroic gesture, it is possible that one might give his life for a just person. Rare as it may be, such sacrifice does occur. But would one die for a person who is unjust, guilty of serious misdeeds, one sentenced to death for his crimes? This is exactly what Christ did for us. With that major step taken, which has resulted in our being made just before God, it is logical to believe that we will be brought to final salvation as well. Our hope, then, is in no way foolhardy or groundless. At this point Paul explains how this gift of God in Christ has been realized (5:12–20).

Adam stands on one side and his "descendants" with him—sin, death, and the law. Once Adam sinned, death entered the world. His sin was the result of transgressing a divine precept, a type of the Mosaic law yet to come. Adam did not act out of ignorance, contravening the divine will without knowing it. On the contrary, there was a very specific precept that he violated. When the law of Moses appeared at a much later date, it became an ally of sin and death inasmuch as it offered humanity the opportunity to specify its malice in again violating specific precepts. History supplies ample proof of the law's ineffectiveness as a force for good. Instead of contributing to human righteousness, the law only made sin more abundant. This debit side of the accounts represents the patrimony received from Adam.[4]

The gift of God, however, far surpasses the evil inherited from the past. Christ is Adam's counterpart as well as his antithesis, with his patrimony of grace and life seen as total gift. He overcomes sin, death, and the law in bringing the gift of the Spirit, which results in authentic and lasting life as well as freedom from the law and its death-dealing consequences. If the action of one person brought condemnation to all, so the action of another has brought acquittal. The benefits from Christ are superabundant, because he is the antidote not only to Adam's sin but the sins of all who followed him and in some way ratified his original transgression. Paul's parallel is complete: on the one side stand sin, condemnation, and death; on the other, grace, justification, and life.

Romans 6. In the sixth chapter Paul speaks of the transition that takes place in baptism and the moral consequences that flow from it. Every baptism is a death. There is no way that one can share in the life of the risen Christ without first experiencing his death, and this occurs in baptism itself (6:1–4). The symbolism itself underscores the reality. Submersion in the pool of water symbolizes burial in the tomb with Christ; it is a form of death embracing within its ambit sin and the law. Baptismal death spells the end of all that has gone before as one rises to newness of life. To acquire this patrimony derived from Christ, the Christian must be divested of Adam's "baggage." In terms that are ontological and not merely morally persuasive, the baptized person is no longer a partner of sin. To revert to sin would be to revert to a former existence, and that makes no sense. As Christ died once for sin and now lives for God alone, so too must the Christian (6:5–14).

Yet it might be argued that since sin and law no longer exercise dominion over us, we can be quite indifferent and even embrace violations with impunity. Paul rules this out on the basis of our new allegiance. Formerly we stood on the side of sin, which led to condemnation and death. Now, however, obedience goes to God, leading to righteousness and life, and any commitment to God in the new order of things precludes a return to or a "dabbling" in the old regime. Yes, Paul states, the person remains always a slave whether in the old order or the new. But between the two types of slavery there is a notable difference. The former era paid "wages" for submission, summarized in the single word "death." The new slavery does not pay wages; it confers only gifts, clearly unmerited and beyond any human attainment, namely, life in Christ Jesus (6:16–23).[5]

Romans 7. What is to be said, then, about the Mosaic law woven so inextricably into the fabric of the former covenant? Paul next turns his attention to this question. For Paul, the principle is clear enough. Just as the new allegiance does not permit a reversion to sin as a master, so too the law belongs to the past and has no role in the life of the baptized. Paul uses the marriage comparison (7:1–6). A woman is bound to her husband for as long as he lives; once he is dead she is free. At this point the parallel shifts somewhat. The Christian becomes the one who has died, but the main point remains intact: death is the point of severance, bringing freedom from the determining law. With his or her baptismal death, the Christian is freed from any obedience to the law. What possible good could the law provide? Speaking in his customary categories of diametrical opposites, Paul states that it was while we were in the "flesh" that law took advantage of our weakness to inflict sin and death; now that we are in the "spirit," the law is as alien to us as is sin itself. In Paul's ontological categories to revert to law is to revert to sin; we now live a new life free from all that is past.

But a certain corrective is necessary here lest Paul find himself misunderstood (7:7–12); there is a fundamental question that cannot be skirted. How can the Mosaic law, enshrined as Torah and central to the covenant through centuries of Jewish history, be an evil? Paul responds to the question unhesitatingly. The law in itself is good and God-given. But sin has used it for its own purpose, to bring about death. As soon as the law appears, sin takes on new life and sees a way of drawing the "children of Adam" into its clutches. The very prohibition expressed by the law becomes an avenue for weak unaided human "flesh" to specify its evil inclination, thus bringing sin to life. Certainly the law in itself is good, Paul affirms, but how else do I know what sin is unless the law tells me? That which is holy and sacred becomes for the weakened "flesh"-bound person a determined way to espouse evil.

And so the law only adds to our moral quandary. Sin wants to use the law, good in itself, for its own end, that is, to produce spiritual death. The law is good, the law is spiritual, but the unredeemed are weak and carnal. Left to his own resources, the generic "I" in Paul's description of the pre-baptismal state (7:13–25) can see the goodness of the law while repeatedly violating it. Mentally "I" know the right and understand the law's provisions but am totally incapable of complying with its directives. Sin is at work within "me" in using the law as a means to draw "me" closer to death. Is there no escape? Yes, in the power and freedom from sin afforded in Christ Jesus.[6]

THE PRIMACY OF LOVE

It is clear that for Paul freedom is not equated with an unbridled license or a self-serving inversion of values. The Spirit has replaced the law as the center of the covenant relationship; but, as Paul insists, this produces its own type of allegiance, willingly embraced, to be sure, but a form of servitude nonetheless. The Spirit is operative in one law only, and that is the law of love. The statement of Galatians could not be clearer: "For you were called for freedom. But do not use this freedom as an opportunity for the flesh; rather serve one another through love. For the whole law is fulfilled in one statement, namely, 'You shall love your neighbor as yourself'" (5:14). It is in response to the Spirit's dictate of love that the concerns of the law are not disregarded but fulfilled. In going beyond the law, the concerns of the law are adequately addressed. But with its far-reaching, positive agenda, love is not circumscribed by the parameters of any law. "The fruit of the Spirit is love, joy, peace, patience, kindness, generosity, faithfulness, gentleness, self-control. Against such there is no law" (Gal 5:22f.). When the desire of virtue is the driving force, the horizons are limitless, with no law-imposed boundaries.

Moreover, as Paul sees it, the higher includes the lower, the greater includes the lesser. To be totally engaged in the law of love is to know that the prescriptions of the law will necessarily be fulfilled. It is the question of a response on a higher key:

> Owe nothing to anyone, except to love one another, for the one who loves another has fulfilled the law. The commandments: "You shall not commit adultery; you shall not kill; you shall not steal; you shall not covet" and whatever other commandment

65

there may be, are summed up in this saying (namely), "You shall love your neighbor as yourself." ...Love is the fulfillment of the law. (Rom 13:8f.)

For Paul, two decisive attitudes toward law make the difference between the old and the new dispensations. What had been itself initially a grace, a divinely established means of responding to the God of covenant, had become a means of reaching or attaining an end. It was not only the Mosaic law but its later additions and modifications that led to a form of legalism antithetical to the work of Jesus.[7] The basic truth is that salvation is not to be achieved; it is to be received. It is, in short, pure gift. The Spirit, the source of justification and the pledge of final salvation, elicits its own response, which is one of love. In the light of new life received, which is justification, the Christian's grateful response will more than satisfy the concerns of the law. In Pauline thought, therein lies the difference between the two eras. Can there be some kind of a convergence, a coexistence of the Spirit and the law? By no means. There is one cause of justification and salvation, and that is faith in the saving work of Christ. To admit of any competing factor is nothing short of blasphemy (Gal 2:16; Rom 3:28). Salvation consists not in seeking justice but in living it.

Divergent Views. What is interesting, however, is that this attitude toward the law is not uniform in the New Testament. While it certainly reflects the posture of Gentile Christianity, the same cannot be said of Jewish Christians. The important decision taken at Jerusalem regarding the law (Acts 15; Gal 2:1–10) freed Gentile Christians from its observance but not Jewish Christians. This goes a long way toward explaining the two distinctly different views on the law that appear in the New Testament. The church to which Matthew's gospel was directed was Jerusalem oriented. Composed for people who to a considerable extent had come from a Jewish background, the gospel is marked by a strong sensitivity to Jewish concerns, even while experiencing hostility from Jewish quarters. For example, the continuing validity of the law for Christian converts appears clearly in Matthew's sermon on the mount (chaps. 5–7). While it is unquestionably true that in the examples cited the Christian fulfills the law in going beyond it, there is very clear emphasis on the abiding and continuing force of the Jewish law (5:17–20). As the evangelist saw it, the Mosaic law was to have validity until the summing up of history with the return of Christ. When he goes on to indicate the way in which the concerns of the law were to be met, he is at one with Paul in stating that it is by going beyond the law. To eliminate all forms of anger from one's life is surely to avoid murder (5:21f.); to turn away from lustful desire is to avoid adultery (5:27f.); to "turn the other cheek" and "go the extra mile" make obsolete the requirement of a retribution that is just (5:38–42). In all of this the Mosaic law is observed in being subsumed in the higher law of love. But Matthew does not handle the question so deftly that the law fades from consideration. He upholds the permanent value of its many precepts, and there is no reason to believe that the community for which he wrote was any less observant of the prescriptions of Torah than its Jewish forebears. It is important to note also that the early church lived with the expectation of an early return of Christ, to be preceded by the Jews' acceptance of his reign.

It is certainly true that this Matthean view of the law did not prevail; it is the thought of Paul that has marked Christian tradition. Historical circumstances were partly responsible for this. The destruction of Jerusalem and its temple, coupled with the overall failure of Judaism to accept Christ, made the law regarding Hebrew ritual and cult increasingly obsolete for Jewish Christians. The development of a distinctly Christian cultic life and an ethic of universal inclusion eventually highlighted an incompatibility with Jewish tenets.

Jesus and the Law. Is it possible to determine the attitude of the historical Jesus toward the law and Jewish tradition? The Christian faith overlay of the gospel tradition makes this difficult to achieve, but it certainly would appear that Jesus maintained a basic respect for the Mosaic tradition. His problems seemed to have centered more on the plethora of precepts that had been added to it. At the same time, the strong sense of personalism that Jesus brought to so many situations often forced him to bypass legal prescriptions when the needs of the individual took precedence. That he presented an ethic which transcended the law, while not generally disregarding it, seems certain from independent sources, such as Matthew and Paul, and at least paved the way for the eventual decision to move away from the Mosaic law as a keynote feature of the church.

It is precisely this point, the centrality of the law of love, that serves to unite the two varying points of view in the early church. While Matthew may be at pains to uphold respect for the Mosaic law, he and Paul concur in seeing the summary of the Christian life in the great commandment of love (Mt 22:34–40). It is in making this the centerpiece of their life that the righteousness of the disciples will surpass that of the scribes and Pharisees (Mt 5:20). But this note of convergence and divergence within the New Testament shows the extent to which the scriptures themselves evidence a gradual growth in understanding. It is only when one views the Bible as a monolith written in some sort of cultural vacuum that this gives rise to surprise. In fact, what the scriptures reflect in their entirety is a revelation that is ongoing and developing, taking measured steps forward as it works through the mindset and beliefs of a people at given moments of their history.

What emerges most clearly in the ethic of the new covenant is its emphasis on the positive response rather than the negative transgression. The penitential rite of the liturgy captures it well as we ask forgiveness for "what we have done and what we have failed to do." In fact, it is the law-respecting Matthew who presents us with the scenario of the final judgment (25:31–46). It is not on violations of the decalogue that the Son of Man dwells in that final summing up but on the law of charity. The new covenant morality asks to what extent the Christian has listened to the Spirit in feeding the hungry, in clothing the naked, in visiting the incarcerated. This goes well beyond any circumscribed legalism and is the moral criterion of Christian discipleship.

THE UNFOLDING TRUTH

People who take a literalist approach to the Bible register concern when conflicting points of view emerge. If the one all-knowing God has revealed the whole of the Bible, then a uniformity of truth is inescapable. Contradictory points of view are unthinkable, since God cannot possibly be at odds with himself. Yet such a view fails to see that the scriptures themselves are an incarnation, wrapped in various times and cultures, with all the limitations imposed upon human authors, even those conveying a divine message. It is sufficient to look at the differing attitudes toward the Mosaic law. Sacred truth was grasped at any given moment to the extent that it was possible. Insights had to go through a process of refinement before they were finally distilled. The knowledge of divine truth was not a blinding flash of light; in every instance it was a gradual process. This has long been evident to students of doctrinal development in the history of the church; it is interesting to note that it is true of the Bible as well.

There are more than enough examples to bear this out. The universalism present in the post-exilic book of Jonah hardly matches the exclusivism of Ezra and Nehemiah. A retribution theory that saw prosperity as a reward for virtue and suffering as punishment for sin, vigorously espoused in Proverbs and Sirach, is seriously challenged by the authors of Job and Qoheleth (Ecclesiastes). And as we have seen, it took no small amount of time for the early church to work though the question of the ongoing validity of the Mosaic law in light of the new era of grace. In all cases the eventual solution was found but only when thesis and antithesis coalesced in a common synthesis. Therein lies the inerrant character of the Bible; it is a God-given guide to life that emerged only after a lengthy struggle resulting from human limitations.

Yet for those engaged in the human enterprise on any level, this is more a consolation than a cause for concern. How else are the enigmas of life dealt with? Truth is a process in many areas of our life, and it is not always easily won. It sometimes takes contrary, even contradictory ingredients to bring us to that eventual synthesis. The scriptures tell us that God deals with us as we are, with divine truth undergoing the same process as any other. We walk between the Scylla of seeing the Bible as a body of revealed truths and the Charybdis of a purely human composition, nothing more than historical speculation on the ultimate questions. We are all too aware that in addressing many issues today we lack the clarity we would like; our answers to many questions, doctrinal and ethical, are provisional at best. We not only struggle with the truth; we also struggle for it. Our scriptural experience tells us that this should come as no surprise.

BEYOND THE LAW

The New Testament converges around the point that grace carries us far beyond the law. It is unfortunate that so much of Christian morality traditionally focused on a decalogue ethic, which ultimately remained only the outer limits of human conduct. The real call of the Christian disciple is to a positive, ongoing response to the God of the covenant, whose overriding love is reflected in the death of his Son.

Unfortunately, the times in which we live show little or no regard for even a decalogue morality. Respect for life at every stage is frequently disregarded. It is violence not peacemaking that abounds. Permissive attitudes toward human sexuality preempt family values. Theft, deception, and double dealing command more attention than divesting oneself of one's coat for another, going the extra mile, or turning the other cheek. This being the case, the moral conscience of society, arising from church or whatever quarter, is so totally absorbed in dealing with its basic ills that we hear very little about the moral imperatives connected with the sermon on the mount. All of this is indeed a sad commentary on our culture, but it is also a reproach to that part of us which is church. The more we relegate the law of charity with its own demands to the life of the "do gooders" or the very special Christians, the more the salt and light that church is called to be loses its savor and its brilliance.

The New Testament harbors the belief, which modern sophisticates may well call naive, that when people are working to better their neighbors' lot, they are much less likely to do them violence. It holds that if I am willing to make a loan without interest to someone in need, sometimes even without repayment, then theft is not likely to emerge at some point as part of my life. It means that if a person gives of his or her time to provide for the needs of pregnant teenagers or single parents, the likelihood of that person's seeing abortion as an option in unwanted pregnancies is reduced immensely. But the point is that in pursuing these positive objectives we are not only avoiding sin but are bringing to society a different perspective. We promote a world wherein the pursuit of positive values, while never totally eliminating sin and its consequences, points clearly to the significance of what God's love for the world means. It elevates to a new level the entire discourse on the dignity of the human person, the sacredness of the environment, and the promotion of social justice. This is what the new covenant is all about.

Lord God, may every eucharist be for me a moment of covenant renewal, a moment of rededication to you and your Son. Deepen within me the conviction that every mass brings to life the death and resurrection of Jesus, the lasting reminder of how far covenant love has carried you. Help my response to be generous and open-ended, marked by a willingness to love you and my neighbor without limit. Make of me the salt of the earth and the light of the world. Amen.

FOR STUDY AND DISCUSSION

1. Discuss the development of the covenant from Sinai to the New Testament.
2. Discuss the relationship between the Sinai covenant and the eucharist. Between Passover and eucharist.
3. Was the Last Supper a Passover meal?
4. What is the origin of the words of institution found in the synoptics' eucharistic narrative?
5. Discuss the eucharist as a sacrifice and meal.
6. "One bread, one body." Explain the relationship between eucharist and church.
7. Explain the controversy regarding the law at the assembly of Jerusalem (Acts 15).
8. What was Paul's attitude toward the law as reflected in Romans 5–7?
9. What is the relationship between baptism and the new covenant?
10. Distinguish between Christian freedom and license.
11. Explain how love is the fulfillment of the law.
12. How do Matthew and Paul differ in their approach to the law? What do you think Jesus' attitude was?

THE NEW COVENANT AND THE JEWS

"Then shall you know that I, the LORD, am your God,
　　dwelling on Zion, my holy mountain;
Jerusalem shall be holy,
　　and strangers shall pass through her no more.
And then, on that day,
　　the mountains shall drip new wine,
　　and the hills shall flow with milk;
And the channels of Judah
　　shall flow with water:
A fountain shall issue from the house of the LORD,
　　to water the Valley of Shittim....
But Judah shall abide forever,
　　and Jerusalem for all generations." (Jl 4:17–18, 20)

The earliest Christian community faced a variety of questions, not the least of which was the future role of Israel. There was no way to read the Hebrew scriptures without being faced with the fact that the final era had to include the people of the Mosaic covenant. These were the people of the promise; the addition of others was a complement, not a substitute. This expectation is seen in the ties to the temple maintained by the first disciples in the period immediately after the resurrection (Acts 2:46, 3:1). The belief in the early return of the Lord was coupled with that of the acceptance by the Jewish people of the covenant fulfillment realized in Christ. Only with the passing of time, with the split between church and synagogue, and the growth of the church in the Gentile world, did the belief in Israel's conversion at an early date tend to recede.

The Jews in the Plan of God: Romans 9–11

It is the apostle Paul, so much at odds with many of his earlier co-religionists' tenets, who alone gives extended consideration to Israel's role in the ultimate plan of God (Rom 9–11). In Romans this follows shortly after his discussion of the superiority of the era of grace over that of the law, of Christ over Adam (Rom 5–7). Since the weight of God's favor has now fallen on the new covenant people, how then explain the fate of Israel? Have the people of the promise been definitively rejected? How explain the favored lot of the Gentiles? Has it been gained at the expense of the people who were uniquely God's own? Paul examines the question in these chapters of Romans and in typical rabbinic fashion freely adapts the scriptures to support his conclusions. It is a fascinating part of Pauline theology, with important implications for Jewish-Christian relations today.

The Election of the Jews. The failure of the majority of Jews to respond to Jesus has caused Paul profound pain (Rom 9:1–5). In the interests of his former co-religionists, Paul goes so far as to say that he would sacrifice his own election and salvation. His sentiments bear a striking resemblance to those of Moses, who in pleading forgiveness for his people is willing to see his own name stricken from the book of God's elect (Ex 32:32). In reflecting on Israel's impressive history, Paul lists seven ways in which the people have experienced God's favor: adoption, glory, covenant, law, worship, promises, and patriarchs. In being *adopted,* Israel became part of God's family, repeatedly referred to as God's son (Ex 4:22; Hos 11:1). Israel was exposed to Yahweh's *glory* in the theophany of Sinai (Ex 19), the cloud and pillar of fire (Ex 16:10), and in the destruction of those who were hostile to God's people (Ex 14:17). It was in the *covenants,* both that with Abraham and that mediated by Moses, that God's favor was singularly manifest. This was the bond that stood at the heart of the God-people relationship and represented Israel's strongest claim on the future. The *law,* an integral part of the Sinai covenant, was historically viewed as a grace, not a burden, an authentic path to life that Israel was privileged to walk. It is a view with which Paul in his newfound freedom will take strong issue, and yet he unhesitatingly lists it as an important part of the patrimony. *Worship* refers principally to temple cult, the setting in which Yahweh's presence was singular. To stand "in his presence" or "before his face" was worship different from any other form of prayer. Finally, God had prepared the way for this definitive moment in salvation history through the *promises* made to the *patriarchs,* especially Abraham, Isaac, and Jacob (e.g., Gn 12). The promise made to David centered on the permanence of the kingship (2 Sm 7:7–11) and was seen as more directly related to Christ. Moreover, the Jews have been favored in Christ himself, who stems from them but whom ironically they have failed to claim.

God's Freedom. Considering this favored status, Paul asks himself how the present situation is to be explained (Rom 9:6–29). Who are the authentic inheritors of the promise? Scripturally, Paul argues, it is not a question of generic descent (vv. 6–13), because not every descendant of Abraham was assured Yahweh's singular blessing. It was upon Isaac and his progeny that the promise was bestowed, not others of Abraham's line (Gn 21:12). And there was a further narrowing within Isaac's line: free election falls upon Jacob, while Esau is disenfranchised. It is election and promise that take precedence over lineage. Therefore, with the dawn of the final era in Christ, it should come as no surprise that some Jews are elected and others are not.

According to Paul's thinking, to judge the action of God by a human yardstick is totally inappropriate (Rom 9:16–24). To say that he is unfair is to deprive him of that freedom of choice necessary for the fulfillment of his plan. Israel was freely chosen so that the mercy of the Creator would be made manifest (Ex 33:19). Moreover, Pharaoh was chosen, not because of any personal worth, but that through his downfall God's love for the insignificant Israel might appear more clearly. In all of this God remains totally free, and God's mercy is the overriding attribute.

Where then do election and human freedom come together? Are people culpable for rejecting something for which they are not chosen? Paul makes no attempt to deal with this question on a quid pro quo basis. God's ways are not those of humans, nor are his ways always comprehended by mortal beings. To illustrate the point, Paul draws on the prophet's image of the potter and the clay (Jer 18) in pointing up the folly of questioning the divine

74

plan. That God is not capricious but patient and forbearing is amply attested in his willingness to bear with evildoers so that his mercy may be ultimately seen. He bore with Pharaoh for the good of the Israelites that the latter might see the power and glory of their delivering God. Throughout history God repeatedly endured evildoers for the good of the elect and their salvation. It is a deliverance that has gone far beyond the Exodus in embracing Jew and Gentile as members of the new covenant. Theological questions may remain unanswered, but the biblical data speaks for itself in upholding the fairness of God.

The Inclusion of the Gentiles. The admission of the Gentiles to the plan of salvation is fully justified as Paul draws on a number of scriptural texts that, although freely adapted, illustrate the divine design. Thus texts that originally spoke of the restoration and reintegration of Israel (e.g., Hos 2:25) are here applied to the incorporation of the Gentiles. In the same way, by citing texts that stretch the intent of the original author, it is shown that a remnant of Israel will always be preserved and become an integral part of the body of the elect (Rom 9:27ff.; Is 10:22f.; Is 1:9). Yet these same texts in their original sense speak of the punishment inflicted upon Israel for her disbelief. This type of interpretation, while quite foreign to the modern critical mind, was common in the Pauline era. In the interests of pointing up the significance of events as part of a divinely orchestrated plan, the scriptures played an essential part in validating that plan. There was one overarching principle in theological investigation: If it's not in the scriptures, it's not in the world.

Paul returns to the thesis of faith over the law as he concludes the first part of his presentation. Never to be overlooked in Paul's eyes is the fact that the Jews failed because they tried to attain righteousness through law observance, whereas the Gentiles accepted it in faith as total gift. In their preoccupation with the law, the Jews "stumbled" over the "saving" stone, faith in Christ, whereas the believer has been led to justice.[1]

The Failure of the Jews. The heart of his discourse brings Paul face to face with the central question: How explain this failure to believe on the part of Paul's own partners in the faith? Certainly righteousness or justice before God stands at the very center of faith (Rom 10:1–4). It is this that all are seeking, whether Jew or Gentile. But the avenue to righteousness has now appeared in Jesus and is extended freely to those who believe. The entire law, indeed all of God's dealings with his people in the past, has pointed to Jesus. The law takes its meaning from Christ, who is in fact the justifying agent, the end of the law itself. To ignore this gift in not accepting faith-righteousness and to continue on the frustrating path that seeks righteousness through law observance is an exercise in futility. It strives for something that is unattainable and fails to recognize the gift. This is the greatest folly.

The Unusual Turn of Events

For Paul, the overriding issue revolves around that fundamental question of law or faith. He never questions the Jews' zeal or their desire to come to the truth, but he has serious questions about their inability to see how incongruous their stance is. The righteousness that God confers is found in Christ. Since all of the law ultimately points to him, to accept him in faith is to bypass the law and to receive uprightness as gift. In a very few words this is the heart of the Christian approach. The Jews, on the other hand, fail to accept Christ and continue to apply themselves assiduously to perfection through the law. In Paul's eyes their approach is doomed to failure.

At this point Paul points up the difference between the two covenants in terms of exertion and acceptance (Rom 10:5–13). In a free adaptation of texts from Leviticus, Deuteronomy, and the Psalms, he builds his case. A righteousness derived from the law, as Moses himself admits, comes from performance; it is a matter of doing. But the justice that comes from faith is not a matter of accomplishment, here expressed in terms of real exertion. Admittedly it was through Christ being born, dying, and rising again that justification became a possibility; yet that was divine, not human, effort. What mortal is able to bring about an incarnation or a resurrection? It is a question that can hardly be raised.

The Closeness of Salvation. As Deuteronomy suggests (30:14), salvation is proximate and intimate. It is a salvation close at hand.[2] All that is required is the full acceptance in the heart and the expression in word of the lordship of Jesus. He is the living Lord inasmuch as God has raised him from death, and to acknowledge him as Lord is to give him the title and allegiance proper to Yahweh alone. This is certainly a quantum leap forward and is possible only in faith, but in the simple and most direct terms, justification and salvation are as close as the heart and the lips. This faith formula expressed in the "Christos-Kyrios," Christ as Lord, was evidently the earliest form of Christian baptism (Acts 2:38; 10:48). Standing at the center of Christian belief, it is a formula that expresses a deep sense of commitment, a willingness to let one's life be fashioned by all that Christ stands for. It signifies a willingness to let the sovereignty of God's reign, with Christ at its center, become the focus of one's existence. It is, moreover, a faith in Christ as Lord of all, open to those who invoke him; thus any barriers of ethnicity, social status, or gender fade into insignificance (Rom 10:12f.; Gal 3:28). It is interesting to note that it is this faith in the Lord Jesus that produces the totally egalitarian spirit of the Christian life.

Paul then looks at possible objections. Can the Jews be culpable if the message has never reached them? The Apostle outlines four steps for the faith to reach the hearer: the mission, the proclaimer, the message, and its reception. In the case of Christ, all four conditions have been met, a fact Paul illustrates with a number of freely adapted scripture texts that bolster his argument. The scriptures themselves indicate that the message has been preached everywhere. It is only because Israel has remained a "disobedient and contentious people" that it has not turned to Christ (Rom 10:21).

THE FUTURE OF ISRAEL

Paul's disparate points of view on his former co-religionists are disconcerting in various ways. The rhetoric is unquestionably honest and is as evenhanded as Paul's character will allow. But the truth of the matter is that it does not easily lend itself to ecumenical dialogue. The most positive turn appears in the latter part of his treatment of the question wherein he speaks of the future outcome. He speaks first of the remnant of Israel that has already espoused the new covenant (Rom 11:1–10) and of the final integration of Israel before the end (11:11–24). The present obduracy of the Jews should in no way be construed as a terminal condition, nor does it suggest their rejection by God. First of all, what the masses have not yet attained, the remnant has. Amply predicted in the Hebrew scriptures, it is illustrated in the example of the prophet Elijah, who when faced with the widespread infidelity of his time was assured that seven thousand faithful Israelites would be spared (1 Kgs 19:18). It is this idea of God's fidelity to his promise in preserving a segment of the population, a vital scriptural datum, upon which Paul builds. In doing so he links it with the concept of God's favor, which finds expression in his steadfast fidelity to his covenant commitment, the faithful remnant being the beneficiary. What the people as a whole *worked* to achieve and did not attain, the remnant was *gifted* to receive.

The Happy Fault. Yet, as Paul reminds his audience, the end has not yet been reached. The temporary failure of the Jews to acknowledge Christ has worked to the benefit of the Gentiles. If this transgression on the Jews' part has resulted in such a blessing, one can hardly imagine the benefit that will be derived from their ultimate obedience to God. Drawing on horticultural imagery, Paul sees no disintegration in the sturdy roots of Judaism. In the first Jewish converts the tree has produced healthy fruit. In giving Christianity its divine and irrevocable past, it has given ample evidence of its vibrant and healthy roots. This positive assessment lends itself to the well-founded hope of what the future will bring. The Jews' ultimate incorporation into the Christian faith will mean nothing less than "life from the dead" (Rom 11:15).

Future Acceptance. The temporary exclusion of the Jews should lead to no overconfidence on the part of the Gentile Christian community. Attitudes of exclusivism are unwarranted inasmuch as the newly grafted branches (Gentiles) draw their life from the roots of Hebrew faith. If the natural branches could be pruned by reason of their temporary obduracy, so too can those that have been grafted in from an extraneous source. But be assured, if the ingrafting of wild olive branches has brought such consolation, how much greater joy will abound with the restoration of the natural branches to the original trunk from which they sprang!

God's call to the people of his original choice remains valid; it has in no way been revoked (vv. 26–28). Paul leaves no doubt as to the ultimate outcome. The temporary marginalization of the Jews has worked to the benefit of the Gentiles as part of God's plan. The former are presently "God's enemies" for the Gentiles' sake. But the promises made to the patriarchs are still in force and will ultimately be realized. Moreover, the Jews are not singular in their disobedience; the Gentiles in their own time shared in it as well (vv. 30ff.). Yet all of this points up the goodness of God. His mercy and favor now reach all, Jew and Gentile alike, all of which will become evident in time. This summation of the place of all in God's saving plan leads to a concluding hymn of praise in which Paul lauds the incomprehensible goodness of God (vv. 33–36).

THE JEWS AND VATICAN II

October 28, 1965 is a landmark in the history of Jewish-Catholic relations. With the definitive approval of the Vatican II document *Nostra Aetate* on the relationship of the church to non-Christian religions, with particular emphasis on Judaism, a long history of strained relations between Christians and Jews was basically altered and a new era of understanding begun.

Vatican II was an ecumenical council in a different sense than would be understood by the ordinary layman or an adherent to another faith. The council was "ecumenical" in the traditional Catholic sense, as one that touched on areas vital to the "world wide" (Greek: *oikumene*) church. Today, however, the word *ecumenical* has taken on a distinctive meaning connected with achieving unity among the churches and religious confessions. In Christian circles it speaks to the unity among his followers for which Christ prayed (Jn 17:21). The truth of the matter is that Vatican II was ecumenical in both senses. It certainly fulfilled its first function as a council of the universal church, but it was also a council with far-reaching effects for other Christian churches and communities of faith. Not only were respected Protestant and Jewish authorities present for all four sessions, but the ecumenical statements of the council launched a new era in mutual understanding and collaboration.

A History of Mistrust. As the inaugurator of the council, Pope John XXIII intimated early on to his trusted collaborator, Cardinal Augustin Bea, that he wanted from the council a statement on the Jews. Bea stated this publicly in an intervention on the council floor on November 19, 1963. There were good reasons for this. The long history of difficulties between Christians and Jews certainly had political and social ramifications and was not solely a "religious" question. However, from the Christian side the fires of animosity were stoked by charges of "Christ killers" and deicide drawn from an overly simplistic and prejudiced reading of the New Testament. When difficulties arose between Christians and Jews, the fault was often laid at the feet of Jewish complicity in the death of Jesus, which gave justification to hostile and negative attitudes. Tenets such as these, while not the major cause, can be said to have contributed to the fate of the Jewish people during World War II.

The Arab Question. Other factors at work at the council impeded passage of the Jewish statement. The complicated relations between Arabs and Jews in the Middle East and the feelings of injustice that surrounded the creation of the state of Israel gave pause to any endorsement of the Jews which might be seen as bypassing Arab sentiments. There are flourishing Arab Catholic communities in the Middle East, and their hierarchical representatives at the council were vocal about the political implications of a statement on the Jews.

Lengthy discussion and controversy over the statement on the Jews, which originally was intended as a part of the decree on ecumenism, only served to strengthen the document. It became a central part of a separate decree dealing with the church and world religions; the political questions were put to rest with a strong defense of the strictly religious and apolitical nature of the statement; *Nostra Aetate* was approved with over two thousand affirmative votes.[3]

The Teaching of Vatican II. In its statement on Christian relations with the Jews, the council emphasized the bond that links

Christians and Jews. It is in the faith of Abraham that both find their roots. Certainly the Jews revere Abraham and the patriarchs as their ancestral forebears, but it is the faith of these fathers that remains their lasting memorial; it is precisely that faith in an all-knowing God whose plan for his people unfolds in history that links Jews and Christians. While agreement is lacking on the way that plan was ultimately realized, this cannot blind the two to their centuries-old unity in a common belief as to their origins, much less permit a spirit of hostility and division. For its part, Christianity has always seen in the Exodus-covenant experience of the Israelites a foreshadowing of its own salvation in Christ.

While many factors explain the history of animosity that has so often characterized Jewish-Christian relations, the failure to recognize rootedness in a common faith remains an overriding enigma. These were not two peoples unrelated on the level of God's revelation; there was much more that united them in God than could divide them in the vicissitudes of human history. We "have come to share in the rich root of the olive tree" (Rom 11:17–20). Moreover, was not the work of Christ directed toward this: the elimination of the wall that separates us (Eph 2:14–16)? Even though the disturbing hostility that often divided Jews and Christians cannot be placed solely at the door of one party, as the document itself honestly states, nonetheless to understand the New Testament is to recognize the weight that is attached to bringing all peoples together, especially Jews and Christians. To live in a religious climate that lets the wounds of separation fester is anomalous at best.

Much of what the council states regarding the Jewish people is a restatement of Paul's teaching in Romans. There is the litany of Israel's favors (Rom 9:4–5) and the recall of the fact that all of the central figures in the birth of Christianity—Jesus, Mary, Paul, the apostles—came from Jewish stock. The council takes a very evenhanded approach to what is certainly a two-sided question. It recognizes that the greater number of Jews did not accept Christ and that some actively opposed the spread of the Christian message. In calling for "mutual understanding" (no. 4, par. 7) the council fathers express the hope that future dialogue and reconciliation will come from both parties (not unmindful of the negative bias that can also be found in Jewish literature). One of the early steps taken on the path of this new spirit was Paul VI's thoroughgoing revision of the prayer "For the Jewish People" (formerly "For the Conversion of the Jews"), which is part of the Good Friday liturgy.

The council in fact nowhere speaks of the eventual conversion of the Jews, as was done in an earlier draft of this document. Rather, it prays for that day when "peoples will address the Lord in a single voice and 'serve him with one accord'" (no. 4, par. 6). It is certainly true that Christian unity is directed irrevocably to the universal recognition of Jesus Christ as Lord and Savior. However, to speak in such explicit terms in a document primarily geared to reconciliation and healing certainly hinders rather than helps. The object of the council's prayer is muted but honest: the coming together of Jews and Christians in the recognition of God as a common Father with an openness that will let the divine plan of unity unfold. Short of an acknowledgment of Jesus Christ, there are countless ways in which a shared heritage can bring Jews and Christians together.

The Death of Jesus. In this healing process the statement of the council on responsibility for Jesus' death has far-reaching consequences. As indicated above, there is no doubt about the fact that negative sentiment regarding the Jews often leaned on their culpability for the crucifixion. The council decisively rejects the label of "Christ killers" as applied to the Jewish people as a whole. The council states that the language of the gospels applies to certain Jews at the time of Jesus and cannot be construed as being applicable to all who came after them (no. 4, par. 7). This is a conclusion wholly consonant with the basic thrust of Jesus' teaching of forgiveness and reconciliation; any notion of a universal curse is totally alien to New Testament thought. However, recent studies on the gospels have clarified the extent to which the problems and attitudes of the early church are reflected in passages and narratives dealing with Jesus' own life. Therefore, in interpreting the text one cannot bypass this *Sitz im Leben* of the early church. The fact that church and synagogue were very much at odds in first-century church life cannot be bypassed in understanding, for example, the negative attitudes toward "the Jews" in John's gospel. This goes beyond the rejection of Jesus in the Johannine narratives and envisions the experience of the early church as well. None of this is to deny the basic conciliar teaching against an "in perpetuum" curse. It would simply state that the gospel narrative has to be understood in a nuanced fashion.

A CALL TO HEAL

It was in the early 1980s, prior to the demise of the Soviet Union, that I made my first visit to Poland. I traveled from Rome to explore the possibilities of establishing a foundation of our Franciscan Order in that country. While visiting the Krakow area, I made it a point to ensure that a visit to Auschwitz would be part of my schedule. The day we made the trip was dreary and overcast, appropriate enough considering the circumstances. I was hardly prepared for the emotions that swept over me. It was in this place that innocent victims in the millions, most of them Jews, were systematically killed during the Second World War. Their voices are still heard. Upon arrival one sees the maze of railroad tracks, much as in a giant stockyard, where trains arrived daily delivering their human cargo in boxcars, terrified people of all ages. There is the sickening irony of the inscription over the main entrance: "Arbeit Macht Frei" ("Work Makes Free"). The rows of dormitory buildings where people lived in crowded, less than human conditions. The large common showers where unknowing people in massive numbers were not cleansed but gassed. The crematoria where chimneys belched the smoke of scorched human flesh by day and night. And then there were the glass-enclosed exhibits of stacked suitcases from every part of Europe, eyeglasses, personal objects, and, yes, children's dolls with a staring gaze that seems to reflect the fear of their young owners. It was not a customary day of touring, too shattering in its effect to admit of immediate comment. The return trip with the priest who accompanied me was made in silence. The impact of the experience was not dulled as are events of centuries past. This was not a medieval or early Christian tragedy found in musty history texts. This had happened in my own lifetime. While I was a schoolboy in Pennsylvania, these people were dying. They were my contemporaries. Many of them would be living today if, for no fault of their own, they had not been destined for an early and dreadful death, solely because of their name or racial origins. This stands as the monumental tragedy of this millennium, visited upon the last century of the era. It all had a numbing effect on me.

Vatican Council II was separated from Auschwitz by less than two decades. But the time for healing had come. The church from the time of the council until today has repeatedly expressed its sorrow for whatever complicity, witting or unwitting, it might have played in such a tragedy. Whatever is to be said for the past, the period since the Second Vatican Council has been marked by steady progress in overcoming hostility and division and in sowing seeds of better understanding and mutual respect.[4]

There is no denying the fact that major doctrinal hurdles separate Christians and Jews. Christians may be divided over particular issues surrounding the message of Christ; Christians and Jews find their major obstacle in the person of Jesus himself. Yet, as the council itself stated, while such important differences cannot be ignored, they need not stand in the way of appreciating that which unites us. For Christians, there is the overriding truth that Christ came to reconcile and to break down dividing walls. And if the present age cries out for anything, it is the elimination of divisions stemming from exaggerated nationalism, religious prejudice, and racial and cultural differences. Long after Auschwitz we still witness the spilling of innocent blood in the pursuit of narrow and single-minded interests, a crime that cries to heaven like the blood of Abel. The tragic results of hatred in this present century have left a permanent scar on the face of all humanity.

All of this can only be seen as a challenge for the world's major religions, which, as voices of God in the world, are called to be agents of reconciliation. This is especially true of the two religions that share a common heritage. Jews and Christians read the same scriptures, pray the same psalms, honor the same patriarchs, and heed the same prophets. In a shared listening to the word of God, Jews and Christians find much that challenges them. In reading the Hebrew scriptures, Christians cannot help

84

but see the centrality of Israel in God's plan. In reckoning with the strong note of universalism in the same biblical books, Jews are reminded of the inclusion of all people in the plan of God. In striving for justice in the world, the common task of both faiths, they must together decry any form of discrimination, persecution, or oppression. As George Santayana pointed out, not to learn from the errors of history simply dooms us to repeat them.

In a very divided world there is a crying need for a message of reconciliation and conversion. It is a common covenant that enables Christians and Jews to be a unifying force. The covenant with Abraham and Moses lies at the heart of our common faith. Jeremiah's promise of a new covenant is seen by Christians as fulfilled in Jesus, as the full flowering of a revelation commonly shared, that which fulfills but does not abolish (Mt 5:17). The fact that we are not united in our faith understanding of how this fulfillment was realized cannot overshadow the fact that in a real sense we are all sons and daughters of the covenant.

God of Abraham, you led our father from his homeland to a future distant and unclear. Lead us on our present path, which is winding and unmarked, to that era of peace and harmony characteristic of your reign. At the center of your Son's message is the call to eliminate division and to build unity. We are all destined for that era when the distinction between Jew and Greek, free and slave, male and female will have no significance. Help us in our feeble efforts to come closer together as believers. What we cannot effect you certainly can. We pray that you hasten the day. Amen.

FOR STUDY AND DISCUSSION

1. Discuss the early church's dilemma over the Jews' nonacceptance of Christ.
2. Point out the ways in which Paul sees the Jews as privileged.
3. The Bible says it all. How is this principle illustrated in Paul's use of the scriptures?
4. How does Paul see the good that has come from the Jews' rejection of Christ?
5. What does it mean to "confess with your mouth and believe in your heart" (Rom 10:9)?

6. What does Paul assert about the final outcome in the plan of God?
7. How do you think a devout Jew would react to reading Romans 9–11?
8. Why was Vatican II a major step forward in Jewish-Christian relations? How did the council speak of responsibility for the death of Jesus?
9. In your experience, is there an increase or decrease in anti-Semitism in our society? What concrete steps can we take to strengthen ecumenical relations?

6

CHRISTOCENTRISM

Philip said to him, "Master, show us the Father, and that will be enough for us." Jesus said to him, "Have I been with you so long a time and you still do not know me, Philip? Whoever has seen me has seen the Father. How can you say, 'Show us the Father'?" (Jn 14:8-9)

Without the covenant what would we have known of God? The scriptures themselves indicate that reason alone can give us partial insight. We can at least understand God as the "ground of our being." But that is a far cry from knowing what God is like in himself. That comes only through revelation, making the covenant, then, the great moment of divine disclosure. When Christians ask themselves: What is God like?, there is now only one answer: "God is like Jesus." It is the God who has espoused a people that comes to the fore. Neither in the Old Testament nor in the New Testament does God speak of himself in an isolated, detached fashion. Rather, he speaks in terms of relationship—with the people, with the individual, or with the universe as a whole.

It is not surprising that Jesus is so often seen in the scriptures against the background of Old Testament types. If Christ is truly the fulfillment of the former covenant, then types drawn from the Hebrew scriptures were seen as aptly describing his person and mission. We will consider two of these: the figure of Moses, and that of the temple high priest in the Day of Atonement liturgy. For Paul and the author of Hebrews, both these personalities cast a particular light on Christ and exemplify some aspect of his calling. He not only fulfills the past but far overshadows it and as our window on God gives ever fuller vision. Finally, we shall look at the total picture of this self-disclosure. What, in a word, has God told us about himself? How can we sum it up?

Christ and the Law of Moses. That Christ replaces the Mosaic law is a centerpiece of Pauline teaching; therefore a comparison, and even contrast, between Christ and Moses comes as no surprise in the development of Paul's thought. It is in the second letter to Corinth, however, that his thinking takes a most interesting turn. In the third chapter Paul makes reference to desired "letters of credential," which are evidently being asked of him. Does this reflect a need to authenticate evangelizers and preachers in the primitive church, often beset by "false teachers"? Or does it represent another obstacle placed by opponents of Paul? We shall probably never know, nor is it a matter of great consequence. Whatever the background, Paul sees the Corinthians themselves as his best letter of recommendation (2 Cor 3:1f.). They are a letter written on Paul's heart, a precious gift from God, an open letter for all to read (v. 2). Using the image more broadly, Paul sees them as a letter that belongs to Christ, which is sent by him, and of which Paul is simply a minister (v. 3a). In keeping with the assurance that the new covenant will be deeply internal (Jer 31:31–34), Paul designates the letter's author as the Spirit who writes not on stone tablets but on the heart itself (v. 3b). In short, in both its cause and effect, the new covenant speaks for itself; it produces the proof of its authenticity (and that of its ministers) in the human heart.[1]

In all of this Paul can take no personal credit; it is God who is at work through Christ. How different the new from the old! The former covenant with its law-centered ineffectiveness produced only death; with the Spirit of Christ now at the heart of the new alliance, there is manifest life (vv. 4ff.).[2] In an unusual adaptation of scriptural texts, Paul then contrasts the two covenant eras (vv. 7–18). It is the figure of Moses during the Sinai experience that comes to the fore. As the account appears in Exodus (34:27–35), after an encounter with Yahweh on Sinai, Moses' face became a striking reflection of the divine glory. So brilliant was his face that he could not uncover it in the presence of the Israelites and thus wore a facial veil that was only lifted when he entered the tent to converse with God. In this way he shielded the people from the overpowering brilliance of reflected glory.

The Veiled Face. Paul gives all of this quite a different turn as he centers on the veil and the radiant face. Whatever might have been said originally about Moses' radiance, it was a glory destined to fade and thus can in no way compare with that of the Spirit-covenant, which far surpasses in glory the shadowy types of the past. For Paul, the covenant of law made demands that could never be met and thus led only to condemnation. The new covenant, on the other hand, is pure gift, and with the Spirit's power the good proposed by the law is now within reach.

This means that the veil of Moses is now seen in a quite different light. It was used by Moses in order that his fading glory not be seen, a glory indicative of an era that was passing away. Paul then goes on to another use of the veil metaphor. It now covers the hearts of the Jews and is symbolic of their blindness and obduracy in failing to understand the difference between the two covenants (2 Cor 3:15–18). It is only when one turns to Christ that the veil is lifted; it is the Spirit, not the law, that grants access to God. While the same God is the author of both covenants, it is in Christ, not Moses, that the true glory of God appears. The glory of the past is in no way comparable to that unparalleled window on God that comes in Jesus.

The Unveiled Face. This "shining face" analogy is then directed to the Christian. Since that same Spirit alive in Christ is shared with us, we are called to assimilate it to an ever-increasing degree. As we conform our lives to the pattern he has set before us (2 Cor 3:18; Rom 8:29), in what is termed *metanoia* or conversion, that glory seen in Jesus' face becomes ever more apparent in our own. Because of this new and personal relationship with the God who has become visible in Jesus, we, as Christians, are enabled to grow constantly in virtue, which can be spoken of as the glory of the Lord shining through unveiled faces.

CHRISTUS SOLUS

There is abundant food for thought in Corinthians' "gospel of the glory of Christ...the image of God" (2 Cor 4:4). Torah has taken on new meaning; it is now to be found in Christ, the living image of God. This is a remarkable concretization of New Testament faith. In some ways it is easier to follow a religion of law. Everything is clearly defined; the parameters of moral conduct are in place; future destiny is assured through observance. The danger is, of course, that laws tend to multiply in assuring that nothing be left to chance. But a faith expressed in law is also sterile and uninspiring; it is anchored by its own weight. Christ now becomes the centerpiece of the new covenant. The measure of a moral response to this new dispensation is Christ himself—in his person, in his life, in his teaching. It is a response that is open-ended, rooted not in a set of laws but in the One who first loved us. As the image of God, Jesus is not just an insightful teacher, a learned rabbi or guru; he is the living expression of the invisible God, the will of God in the flesh. "Whoever has seen me has seen the Father" (Jn 14:9). Instead of How should I react in this given situation?, the question is: What would Christ do in this set of circumstances? The response will inevitably fulfill the law but it will go beyond it as well. With the only "yardstick" being the law of love, this will often mean turning the other cheek, going the extra mile, forgiving "seventy times seven times."

The new covenant is truly Christocentric. That focus on Christ alone is never lost in the Pauline letters. "For we do not preach ourselves but Jesus Christ as Lord" (2 Cor 4:5). To introduce law together with Christ would be an inadmissible compromise; the vision must never be blurred. It is for this reason that Paul repeatedly subordinates human authority in the church. Ministry is at the service of the people of the covenant, who belong exclusively to Christ as Christ belongs to God (1 Cor 3:21f.). This is something of which the church must be constantly mindful. Not only are secular values often in competition with the commitment to Christ alone, but within the church itself practices, devotions, and causes, often good in themselves, may obscure the Christian vision. Laws, which are necessary for the church to operate, should be kept to a minimum lest we revert to a religion of practice rather than one of adherence to a person. The Spirit binds us to Christ with the bond of love, and with Christ as our window on God, we are bound to the Father as well. So inestimable is that gift that it should never be lost to sight. That accounts for the Christocentrism of Paul's thought.

Finally, the new covenant represents a process. As we are more and more assimilated to Christ, that image becomes ever more visible in our lives, or, as Paul says, we are being transformed "from glory to glory" (2 Cor 3:18). That gives us something to look forward to just as it challenges us to grow. At the same time, it consoles us when we realize that we are not what we should be. Indeed, this is what conversion or *metanoia* is all about, that ongoing (even if occasionally interrupted) process of growth in love. It is not a question of a greater fidelity in the observance of laws, of rooting out vices because they need to be rooted out, or of using a commandments' "yardstick" to determine where we stand before God. Rather, it is a question of continuing the journey, of meditating on the image of Jesus and all that connotes, and then responding to that One who so convincingly gave his all for us. Most of us would admit that we are not where we would like to be. On the other hand, we are thankful that we are not where we were. For some, growth is more intense; for others, more measured. But what is important is that conversion continue. By this shall people know that we are his; we resemble him more and more. If Christ is the window on God, then our lives should be a window on Christ. It is a window that becomes ever more transparent. In that simple formula is to be found all the hallowed expressions of the past: striving for perfection, growth in holiness, the three degrees of sanctity. It is the inherent dynamism of conversion that brings the new covenant to life.

OUR HIGH PRIEST

While the epistle to the Hebrews does not address the traditional Christian priesthood in an explicit fashion, it is the New Testament book par excellence for reflection on what priesthood means. When it comes to an understanding of the genesis of the epistle, there are more unknowns than knowns in naming the author, the audience, the place of composition, and even why it is designated an epistle. It was certainly part of the church's life by the early second century, and its canonicity has never been seriously questioned. It is much more a pastoral message than a letter, even though its conclusion relates it to the latter. The epistle relies so heavily on Old Testament themes that familiarity with the Hebrew scriptures is evidently presumed, and thus a Jewish Christian audience seems likely. Its attachment to the Pauline corpus was an artificial addendum, and Hebrews today is not included in the literature of Paul.[3]

The uncertainties connected with Hebrews in no way detract from its forceful eloquence in contrasting the two covenants. It is Christ the high priest who is placed in bold relief, and it is from this epistle that the term *priest* enters the Christian vocabulary. It is important to note that, aside from the Jewish priests, the term is applied to no one except Christ in the New Testament. In fact, in Hebrews *priest* in its Christian sense is used with a very strong exclusivity in underscoring the singular character of the new sacrifice and its sole mediator. In chapters nine and ten the covenant theme comes to the fore most forcefully.

Worship of the Two Covenants. Written from a distinctly Christian perspective, Hebrews can see little likeness between the two covenants in bringing about an access to God. Drawing on the depiction of the Mosaic tent of worship (Ex 25–26), the temple's forerunner, the author depicts a worship centered in the outer sanctuary, maintaining a clear demarcation from the inner sanctuary (most holy place) where the high priest entered only once a year. The author highlights the furnishings of both the outer and inner sanctuaries (Heb 9:2ff.) and in so doing underscores the external and ritual character of the worship of the past. In including some of the manna and Aaron's staff with the stone tablets inside the ark, the author exceeds the evidence but effectively builds his case for a plethora of sacred objects connected with the past.

The cult of the former era with its strong focus on the externals proved ineffectual (vv. 6–11). With its relics, purifications, and sacrifices, its exclusivity with reference to the inner sanctuary, and its marked concern with those things that only purify "the flesh," the worship of the past has been clearly overshadowed by the work of Christ. With the exaltation of the new high priest, something unsurpassed has transpired (vv. 11–15). It is the language of liturgy that here replaces that of resurrection-exaltation. Drawing on the Israelite imagery of the Day of Atonement, the author has Christ take his death offering of blood, essential for the forgiveness of sins (v. 22), and pass into the heavenly holy of holies. In making atonement for the sins of his people, he carries not animal blood but his own, the single salutary sacrifice effective for all time. Formerly the high priest entered once a year to atone for his own sins and those of the people with the offering of animal blood; it was an atonement that might be said to be only "skin deep" (flesh). Now Christ enters the heavenly tent only once with the offering of a perpetual sacrifice, not for himself but solely for the people; it is an oblation with deeply internal effects in removing sinfulness and cleansing conscience. The offering of Christ makes of its beneficiaries Spirit-filled and upright worshipers of the living God. The full access to God, excluded by the former covenant, is now readily available to all who benefit from the single and unrepeatable offering of the new high priest.

Blood Rites. The author passes from general considerations of Old Testament types in sacrifice and the Day of Atonement liturgy (Lv 16) to explicit covenant considerations in contrasting the mediation of Moses with that of Christ (Heb 9:15–22). Covenants are established in blood, which means a death has transpired. With a certain amount of overstatement, Moses is presented as sprinkling not only the altar (Ex 24:6) but the book of the law, the tabernacle, and the vessels of worship. This concluded the ritual in which the Sinai covenant was established. Now Christ is the mediating agent of a covenant that encompasses not only the future but the past as well. The ineffective atonement of past offerings is now offset by the all-embracing death of Christ, which takes transgressions of the past within its ambit.

At this point there is an interesting play on the Greek word for "covenant" *(diatheke),* which may also mean "last will or testament." Since a will is not probated until the death of the testator, there is no inheritance while the one making the will is alive. So too the heavenly inheritance, proper to the old and new dispensations, becomes effective only with the death of Christ (vv. 15ff.).

Thus in various ways the covenant that was passing away, with all its figures and types of things to come, has been supplanted by the "better times" that had long been predicted (Heb 9:23–26). The temple sanctuary was a human shadow of the heavenly one; the blood rites that went with the annual offering of the past need not continue in view of the sacrifice of Christ. In a former era judgment for sin followed death; now the death has taken place, sin is abolished, and the faithful await not judgment but deliverance at the return of the high priest.

THE HEART OF CHRISTIAN REDEMPTION

There is a remarkably precise summation of Christian soteriology in the early verses of chapter 10 (vv. 1–10). Again contrasting the two sacrifices, the author, speaking from his Christian vantage point, sees proof for the ineffectiveness of past sacrifices in the necessity to repeat them. He argues that what is remitted requires no further atonement. The constant repetition of sacrifice only illustrates that rather than remove sin, it only brought it to mind (v. 3).

Then, in a free adaptation of Psalm 40:7–9, or what might be termed a process of Christian "rethinking," the author of Hebrews looks critically at the two covenants. "Sacrifice and offering you did not desire, but a body you prepared for me; holocausts and sin offerings you took no delight in" (Heb 10:8). The sense here is different from that of the original psalmist. The author of the original psalm subordinates sacrifice to obedience, whereas the author of Hebrews effectively nullifies all past sacrifice as part of an era that has been superseded; offerings served to point to the future, a function that is no longer necessary. "Then I said, 'As is written of me in the scroll, Behold, I come to do your will, O God'" (v. 7). The second covenant is established with the removal of the first. Sacrifices belonged to the period of the law; it is obedience that makes the single new covenant offering efficacious. The offering of God's Son is the divinely decreed avenue of final and total salvation. This is the Father's "will," and Christ makes it totally his own in a loving submission looking to the salvation of the world. It is the will of Christ attuned to that of the Father that reverses the disobedience of Adam, which primordially launched the entire era of sin and death. The second Adam gives his "yes" to God and the tide of history is reversed. In Christ humanity has responded favorably to God and each generation and individual must make that response actual. In the light of this unsurpassed and unimagined gift of Christ, everything connected with the cult and sacrifice of a former era, as significant as it was in its time, now fades into insignificance.

THE CATHOLIC PRIESTHOOD

In teaching candidates for the Catholic priesthood through the years, I often felt their sense of disappointment when it came to speaking of ministry in the New Testament. There is no lack of data on the exercise of various forms of *diakonia*, but there is precious little on the priesthood as it has developed in the life of the church. The term *priest* itself, as has already been noted, is used only of Christ in an individual sense and of the Christian community as a whole in a collective sense (1 Pt 2:5). The fact is that various forms of ministry have been integrated into our understanding of the role of the priest, with that of presider at eucharist a centerpiece. While it is quite true that early Christianity guarded carefully its designation of Christ as the sole priest of the new era, the fact is that time saw the term applied to other functionaries within the church as well. That being the case, it is important for us to explore the significance of this link. What does it mean to be a priest in the church today?

It is here that the epistle to the Hebrews plays a vital role. Christ's priesthood centers upon his being the sole mediator between God and his people. In being the God-man he bridges the gap between heaven and earth. He brings the word of God—in his person, teaching, life, death, and resurrection—to enlighten humanity on its earthly journey. In his humanity he suffers, agonizes, and carries our burdens, and through his death-resurrection gives us access to the heavenly dwelling place of God. It is in this central dimension of his mission that Christ models the priest of today, or, for that matter, of any age.

The Priest a Sacramental Presence. With the central role of the priest as eucharistic presider in place, we can see both dimensions of this mediating role in the way priesthood has evolved. The priest still has the word of God in its presentation, interpretation, and application as a central part of his life. Being

95

schooled in the word finds him imparting Christ in the pulpit, the classroom, at the sickbed, or wherever that word needs to reach. He is the one through whom the voice of a covenant God touches his people. Needless to say, he is not alone in this. There is the "priesthood of the faithful," which has never been more in evidence than it is today. The postconciliar development of ministries in the church has been an incredible enrichment, and the ministry of the word, especially in teaching, is now more than ever seen as a shared responsibility. Nothing that the priest does should ever diminish this array of gifts.

But the priest remains a leaven within this "mix." Within the community his preparation for ministry enables him to empower and to assist the laity in the exercise of their calling. While he no longer occupies center stage in a dramatic monologue (if he ever should have), the value of his contribution to church life is in no way diminished; on the contrary, it is enhanced. The covenant role from God's side is today multifaceted, but the priest's role remains indispensable. He still speaks the word of divine engagement.

Hebrews tells us that Christ cried out to God "with unspeakable groaning" during his earthly days. If priesthood is a call to be at the service of people and to suffer with them in their trials, then this is but an extension of the mission of Christ. The priest brings the lot of his people before the Lord in intercession and prayer. In fact, it is the ministry of service that stands at the heart of New Testament teaching and is so much to the fore since the Second Vatican Council. This is closely tied to the notion of priestly mediation. There is no question here of status or privilege, so much at odds with the whole of Christ's bearing. Rather, it is a question of sharing burdens, of alleviating pain, of addressing ills. This is why the priest's life is so intimately tied to the eucharist, announcing the death of the High Priest until he comes. With the offering of Christ, the priestly mediator follows his predecessor into the inner recesses of the heavenly sanctuary where God's people are now privileged to stand.

People to God, God to people. This is what priesthood in the new dispensation means. Just as there is only one sacrifice of which the eucharist is an extension, so too there is only one Priest continuing to offer himself through the sacramentality of human agents. Thus it will always be. This is not to prejudice the case for or against the persons to whom the priestly office will be consigned in the future, nor does it predetermine the way in which church praxis will eventually move. The fact remains unchanged. Priestly ministry is sacramental and is essentially covenantal. It does not stand apart or above; it is woven into the texture of the new God-human relationship. It is not an honor that one assumes for oneself; rather, one is chosen from among humans for God to address human concerns. Beset by all the weaknesses of their people, priests, like Christ, are well suited to understand the needs of people and bring them before the Lord. If it can be said to be a sainted life, it is so because of its close identity with Christ himself and the people he has made his own.

GOD'S OUTREACH

What view does our window on God provide? As a covenanted people, the family of God, we are privy to insights that would not have been otherwise possible. At this point in our study of the unfolding plan of God, it remains for us to explore what the covenant God tells us about himself.

As we have seen, the human component of the covenant relationship as seen in the covenant terms varies considerably. There is no single or invariable expression of duties and responsibilities. But what appears clearly in all the covenant accounts is the divine initiative; there would never have been a bond if God had not taken the first step. The Judeo-Christian tradition is not the history of a search for God; rather, it is the Lord himself who designs and executes the partnership. Whether the human actor is Noah, Abraham, Moses, or Jesus, the principal player is God. This notion of a God who draws close to his people evolves and expands as salvation history progresses. "What are humans that you are mindful of them, mere mortals that you care for them" (Ps 8:5)? When we consider the twisted and crooked path that humanity has followed, even with its moments of greatness, this constant pursuit by the "Hound of Heaven" seems anomalous at best. In fact, the repeated failures after the initial engagement only stoked the fires of Yahweh's determination, which was to reach its climactic moment in the coming of Jesus. As we marvel at the extent to which God's concern carried him, how clearly we are reminded that with all our inadequacies we are a people dearly loved. Creation itself is a gift; so is life. But beyond that a fuller life in God gives purpose and meaning to human existence and points as well to a life beyond. The history of covenant development shows that the Christ-event, as unsurpassable as it was, was not uncharacteristic of God; the groundwork had been laid in the many expressions of divine outreach that fill the pages of the Hebrew scriptures. Covenant history cannot help but give us confidence. To paraphrase Romans, if God has gone this distance for our benefit, will he not carry us the last mile as well?

Election and Mission. In any Christian reading, it is this outreach of God that gives meaning to the word *love*. In speaking of the meaning of love, the first letter of John sees it well illustrated in the fact that God sent his son into the world as savior (1 Jn 4:9). Thus both the nature of love and the nature of God are defined in terms of generosity. It is not a love turned in on itself but rather one that is centrifugal which lies at the heart of faith. Christianity is not at odds with a justifiable self love, as the great commandment itself makes clear, yet the noblest meaning of charity comes to rest in the person of Jesus. A love centered solely on self ends in *eros,* whereas it is *agape,* a self-giving love, that dominates the Johannine vocabulary. To begin the Christian discourse with *our* love of God is to reach out and embrace an abstraction. It is because we have been the recipients of love that we are moved to respond. "In this is love: not that we loved God, but that he loved us" (1 Jn 4:10).[4]

It is for this reason that the whole question of mission in the church flows from election. "It was not you who chose me, but I who chose you and appointed you to go and bear fruit" (Jn 15:16). It is only when we realize the extent to which we weak human beings have been gifted and embraced, loved in our inadequacy, that we are moved to bring that message of gospel love to the world. This is the meaning of evangelization, and it is quite distinct from theologizing. Theology may well rest in the hands of people of faith, as it most frequently does; it can thus be well served. But is it essential that a theologian be a believer? The time-honored description of theology as "faith seeking understanding" says it well, but it is "belief" that does the seeking, not necessarily a "believer." One may have a keen understanding of the message and be well skilled in using the tools of theology without necessarily embracing the faith.[5] In short, theology is a discipline governed by its own norms, within the grasp of any who would master it. That both faith and theology are best found in the same person (and in certain cases this is indispensable in terms of church life), would not seem to preclude a real separation of the two in given cases.

But such cannot be the case in speaking of evangelization. It proposes because of conviction; it proceeds from faith and moves toward faith. It begins with the notion of divine outreach and seeks to touch human hearts with that message. It can make use of the results of exegesis and theology, and well it should, but its purpose is not determined by better understanding. It looks to changing lives and moving hearts. If theology may be defined in terms of the human look at God, then evangelization looks to a deeper appreciation of God's attention riveted on us.

It is this notion of God's outreach that gives the Acts of the Apostles such fire and dynamism. Faith moves forward with a geographical expansiveness that overturns the boundaries of ethnicity and culture. The Spirit is the principal actor throughout, even to the extent of pointing out the road the missionaries are to follow (Acts 16:7f.). A Pentecost of Spirit and tongues, as that which inaugurated the Jewish mission in Jerusalem (Acts 2:4), is experienced by the pagan Cornelius and his family in Caesarea (Acts 10:44), with the infant church's continual growth. Through it all the broad embrace of God is placed in strong relief.

Outreach to the Unwanted. It is a covenant God that undergirds the scriptural teaching on Jesus' concern for the unwanted: the tax collector, the adulteress, the sick and abandoned along the road on the journey of life. This is but an extension of the Sinai outreach, a further opening of the window on God. Love speaks the language of exaggeration in the Lucan tryptich: the lost sheep, the lost coin, and the lost son (Lk 15). What human wisdom can be found in leaving an entire flock of sheep unguarded for the sake of one? It makes little sense to undertake spring

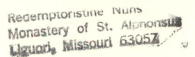

housecleaning to recover an insignificant coin, even if one is poor. And for a father to be so oblivious of justice and fair play by reinstating a ne'er-do-well son with such abandon astonishes the other son and the reader as well. But "my ways are not your ways, says the Lord." This is a God who destroys all barriers, relentlessly pursues the wayward, and disregards human logic at every turn. This does not mean that evil is not suitably addressed and dealt with. Assuredly this is a God who is not mocked. Yet there is no denying the fact that the weight of revelation comes down strongly on the side of mercy and compassion. It is in these terms that the figure of the covenant God is presented.[6]

The scriptural evidence for the outreach of God is virtually inexhaustible. But what is important is to translate that message into contemporary life. Polls repeatedly show that most people in the United States believe in God, and the rate of church attendance, while on the decline, remains quite high. We are not frequently asked to present anew our logical proofs for the existence of God learned in college theodicy. But when one takes that book off the shelf, gives it a good dusting, and sets to "brushing up" on those proofs, it doesn't really say a great deal. While it may lead us ultimately to the God of the scriptures, it certainly does not adequately describe him. Human reason may certainly bring one to the realization that the universe we inhabit is not self-explanatory, that it points to a cause beyond itself. But the recognition of that fact is not an act of faith. The God who is the "first cause" is still a far cry from the God of Abraham, Isaac, and Jacob. In fact, the God of the Bible never waited to be sought out; it was he who took the initiative. And it is that undercurrent of love and concern that keeps erupting in the biblical narrative; it gives meaning to the term *God* and makes a suitable human response an imperative. It is not a question of our reaching God; it is one of realizing that he has touched us.

It is precisely that which we must attest to in our lives. John says repeatedly that it is the community of love that brings God's love to life. Sterile abstractions attract no one, but a sense of concern and outreach will. And it is here that Christians falter. People may never be touched by an argument for God's existence, but they are seldom unmoved by authentic Christian concern.

A Call to the Church. The question with which we are repeatedly faced is whether or not the church presents itself to the world as an extension of Christian compassion and concern. In many ways it does; the record speaks for itself. But today one hears negative reactions to the church, some of which we thought were long ago put to rest. Perceptions often have a way of outliving their accuracy and their helpfulness. The church has long been seen as speaking with clarity on principle and making clear distinctions between right and wrong. While traveling on a sea of relativism and uncertainty, that can be a welcome beacon on the horizon. But on the other hand, unfortunately, many people retain the image of a severe church, unbending and inflexible, which, at least by perception, opts for principle over persons. Some people still believe that there is no place for them in the church because they are divorced. An abortion procured at any stage in one's life spells rejection by God. Homosexuals see themselves as outlawed and abandoned. Admittedly, some misconceptions are present in all of this, but for most people perception becomes the reality. Our point here is that such convictions, whether based on reality or perception, are very much at odds with the overarching message of the scriptures.

It is immensely rewarding to be an agent of mercy because it is so Godlike. That compassion is at times accompanied by the difficult word or the bitter dose may be unavoidable. But it can be cushioned by love. Much depends on the manner in which the message is conveyed. We begin with the premise that there is a place at God's table for everyone, and our greatest pain as Christians is to see someone barred. That is a mindset at odds with any type of exclusivism. We must begin with a sense of inclusivism and then make decisions regarding credentials with a high level of sensitivity.

With all the progress that characterizes our modern age, never have we seen such a high level of alienation. We are beset by psychologically wounded people: single parents, children of divorced parents, victims of physical or sexual abuse. For some young people the only form of social identity they know is that of "the gang." Some people are homebound because of age, illness, fear, or a combination of all three. Increasingly the workplace is

101

where one is seen more as an object than a person, where there is the constant fear of unemployment or the boredom of endless drudgery. Individualism has taken precedence over church or neighborhood as the locus of communion. Fear of crime has driven an even deeper wedge into community spirit. The picture as we know from an even cursory reading of the daily papers is one of a sick and ailing society.

Faith and Indifference. Yet at some point faith has to take hold. We are a covenanted people, a community bonded with God. The mandate is clear: "Do not be conquered by evil but conquer evil with good" (Rom 12:21). It is only when we become detached bystanders that evil has its day. If we are simply onlookers of the world that surrounds us, passive observers of tragedy as life is decimated, people who watch godlessness increase and do nothing, only then do we have cause to fear. A covenanted people has its own apologetic; the holiness of God becomes visible in a holy people. The blueprint for the human response to God's espousal is to be found in the covenant terms; in the new covenant these terms are found in Christ himself. The sermon on the mount is not simply a written document; it is to come alive in the new people of God. To neutralize that teaching through compromise, indifference, or betrayal is to renege on our side of the agreement, leaving the world desolate, barren, and lifeless. When the salt loses its savor or the candle fails to shed its light, then God's promise is not seen as fulfilled, the clarion tones of covenant love are simply not heard.

The extension of God's love is woven into the fabric of outreach. The God of the scriptures was constantly pressing against boundaries and extending the perimeter. The apostolic mandate saw the saving message being carried to "Jerusalem, throughout Judea and Samaria, and to the ends of the earth" (Acts 1:8). Covenant people can never settle on being a comfortable, circumscribed elite. Open to the people of every race and nation, they are especially welcoming to the weak and the dispossessed, the homeless, the unemployed, the illegal alien, the AIDS sufferer. The covenant demands new efforts to reach the unchurched. True, in caring for the active parishioners today there is more than enough work to go around. But what of all those who were once ours and now, for one reason or another, have been lost to view? Misunderstanding, hurt feelings, embarrassment—the causes are multiple, but the people are still ours. And sometimes the remedy can be so simple. A knock on the door, a friendly visit, some sign of concern—these are avenues that can often represent a turning point. If, as we are taught, baptism means both consecration and mission, then we are all missioned. For some this will mean work in a foreign land helping a developing church, but for all it means outreach, the language of covenant in determining ways in which the boundaries of the faith community may be extended. It is the example of Christ that stands out so clearly. Nothing stopped him from reaching out to all, especially the most unattractive. In pursuit of this goal he was willing to set aside provisions of the law and risk the ire of his opponents. When it came to outreach, he was single-minded. As covenant partners we can be no less.

Lord God, in making us your own people you have given us Jesus as the concrete expression of your otherness. To know what you are like, we need but look to him. The picture of your Son is one of compassion, mercy, and forgiveness, as he calls us forth to live a life consonant with our belief. Give us the grace to be covenant partners in looking at the ills of our society not as a symbol of irreversible decadence but as a challenge to bring change and a new spirit to the world that surrounds us. Amen.

FOR STUDY AND DISCUSSION

1. Christ in his life and teaching is the centerpiece of the new covenant. How would you explain this?
2. How do you explain the fact that Moses' veiled face has one meaning in Exodus and another in 2 Corinthians?
3. What does it mean to call Jesus "our window on God"?
4. Discuss what it means to say that our own lives must become an ever more transparent "window on Christ."
5. In the epistle to the Hebrews, Christ is our high priest and our victim. Explain this in the light of Jewish cult.
6. Point out the differences in our understanding of priesthood and sacrifice in the Old and New Testaments.

103

7. The New Testament never uses the term *priest* of any liturgical offi-
   cer. How do you explain that?
8. How does Hebrews 10:1–10 highlight the core of Christian redemption?
9. If we have but one priest and one sacrifice, how do you explain the
   Catholic priesthood and the mass?
10. Divine initiative stands at the heart of biblical covenant. How does
    that affect us as believers, as people missioned, as people to be con-
    cerned for the disenfranchised?

THE SPIRIT AND THE LAW

"Not for your sacrifices do I rebuke you,
nor for your holocausts, set before me daily.
Were I hungry, I would not tell you,
for mine is the world and all that fills it.
Do I eat the flesh of bulls
or drink the blood of goats?
Offer praise as your sacrifice to God;
fulfill your vows to the Most High.
Then call on me in time of distress;
I will rescue you, and you shall honor me."
(Ps 50:8, 12–15)

The pendulum of religion swings back and forth between doctrine and poetry. It is doctrinal clarity that reaches the mind, while poetry and art touch the heart. On one occasion on a flight from Rome to New York I was seated beside an Italian-American lady, well-spoken and educated, who was traveling home with her doctor husband and three children. While her conversation was heavily laden with Catholic insight, I had the distinct feeling that she was of a different faith. My hunch proved to be correct. A few years before the family had joined a fundamentalist Protestant sect, which had since proved much to their liking. Formerly her children had to be almost forcibly led to CCD class once a week where it was "doctrine, doctrine, doctrine"; now class was exclusively Bible, which drew them like a magnet. This contrasted in my mind with the sentiments of my Catholic theology students who, as children of the '70s and '80s, lament the lack of any consistent doctrinal presentation during their elementary and high school years of Catholic training. In the truly Catholic tradition there has to be room for both. We are not simply cerebral believers nor are we nonthinking emotional pietists. While definition and explanation are of singular importance in articulating our belief, it is quite true that it is art, of which the Bible is the prime example, that stirs the soul.

Music, painting, and literature incarnate doctrine and give it a pulsating and energizing quality. They are part of the myth or drama that draws us personally and deeply toward that God who stands at the center of belief. To listen to the *Libera me* of Verdi's *Requiem* is to grasp the yearning of the soul to go beyond the grave; Christ as the spotless Lamb of God is so well depicted in the limpid and pure beauty of the *Agnus Dei* in Mozart's *Coronation Mass.* Who can help but have some experience of what transforming love means in seeing Bernini's sculpture of St. Teresa in ecstasy during a visit to Rome? Faith has to go beyond speculation if it is to touch the heart, and this requires the language of art. The great contribution of a John of the Cross or a Thomas Merton is to have brought the meaning of God to life in poetry. What it may lack in precision is more than compensated in its ability to reach the heart.

The Covenant of the Heart. For the Christian, what Jeremiah speaks of as the covenant written in the heart is realized in that definitive bond inaugurated with Jesus. Particularly interesting is the manner in which it balances individual and communal dimensions of the bond. While Jeremiah never sacrificed the notion of a covenant with a people, his "new alliance" emphasizes the personal relationship between God and the individual. Strongly underscored in the New Testament is the idea of interior renewal, a spiritual rebirth making one a member of the family of God, a sharer in the life of the Trinity, enabling one to call God Abba or Father (Gal 4:6f.). The way scripture expresses this in endearing, even tender language is noteworthy. This is not simply God's choice of a people or the constitution of a theocracy. It says much more in focusing upon an internal transformation, initiated in baptism and continued in the sacramental life of the church, which sets before the believer a new set of values and is at the same time the key to immortality.

The difficulty, of course, lies in keeping this central truth fixed before the eyes of the believer. All religions rely on a certain amount of structure, and most of them strive to articulate their convictions. Karl Rahner expresses it well:

> *Let us imagine that ten people say: "This 'stupid' institutional church is of no interest to us; let's separate from it and found a charismatic and enthusiastic fellowship." At some point someone is going to have to announce: "We are meeting next Tuesday at 5 o'clock, and you my Spirit-filled brothers and sisters must all be there." Then the problem will arise where to get the chairs and where to find the money. Finally someone will have to be chosen treasurer just as it was with Jesus' community. In other words, it won't be long before you have an institutional church."[1]*

Love Over Knowledge. All of this is part of the human side of the equation, and it is quite inescapable. But definition and structure, as necessary as they may be, are not the "glue" that binds us to God. There must be an inherent affectivity in belief to explain sainthood, martyrdom, religious orders, dedicated people. For us to set forth doctrine as an articulation of belief is indispensable; otherwise we are "loose ended" and "all at sea." But to believe that the end of faith is knowing how to explain it, is to lose sight of the personal relationship that underlies it all. Everything must converge on the living God present in Jesus. To give anything else equal status is at best misdirected and at worst idolatrous.[2]

Through the centuries the church has captured her belief in determined formulas or creeds. Without exception, these give valid insights into the mystery of God and God's relationship with the world, humanity, and the church. Yet inasmuch as they are human formulations they never give a comprehensive or total presentation of the truth, a fact that the church itself recognizes when it speaks of its "growth in understanding."[3] This is so because as we approach the transcendent we are dealing with mystery in the fullest sense of the word. Human language can never be raised to the level of an absolute in speaking of the mystery of God. The same is true of the Christian ethic. It is vitally important for the church to speak on moral issues and to give directives for human behavior. This serves as an important bridge between the scriptures and the lived experience of any historical moment. There is, moreover, a hierarchy of moral teaching; some principles are more basic than others. With new developments in science, technology, and the behavioral sci-

107

ences, the church attempts to respond in the light of her own lived experience with the guidance of the scriptures and traditional teaching. In a Spirit-guided church the sincere Christian sees the significance of such directives as pointing to the Supreme Good, the end of human existence.

Yet it is hard to die for a definition or a dogmatic formulation. When one wonders how far faith should carry us, it is always helpful to read the epistle to the Hebrews. In reviewing the vibrant faith of the Hebrew patriarchs (chap. 11), the author cites the example of Abraham. On three noteworthy occasions his faith in a living and personal God carries him to the brink. When told to leave his homeland and move toward the land of promise, he does so with the abandon of a wandering nomad. (In fact, his being landless was in view of the heavenly homeland that was his final destiny.) When, advanced in years, he and Sarah are promised a numberless posterity, the response is one of steadfast confidence. And finally, when told to sacrifice Isaac, the son of promise, he carefully prepares for the offering, reasoning that "God was able to raise even from the dead" (Heb 11:8–19). In citing the patriarchs, the author clearly shows that faith in action is the only faith worthy of the name.

All too often today faith is identified with issues, and there is endless posturing around positions or ideologies. Labels freely attach themselves to people concerned with social problems, orthodoxy, biblical fundamentalism, concelebration, and female altar servers. With increasing frequency new issues emerge around which there is a rallying cry; a "litmus test" of church fidelity often centers on issues of very limited significance. This leads to a splintering within the church and forms of polarization totally at odds with the spirit of the gospel. It is the ageless story of the letter over the spirit, of sacrificing liberty for law, of absolutizing the relative. Christian teachers walk a delicate path between the Scylla of doctrinal maximalism and the Charybdis of an unspecified religiosity. The living and loving Christ must always stand at the center of church discourse. Such may sound platitudinous, but the dangers of focusing solely on particular aspects of church teaching without clearly situating them in a broader context are not inconsequential. It is the covenant of the heart that undergirds acceptance of all teaching. Apart from the love of God that comes to us in Christ Jesus, both acceptance and rejection lose their significance. It is only when this love of God sheds its light upon principles or dogmas that our embrace of the truth has meaning. And if change takes place in our understanding of God's truth, it will be in the light of a clearer perception derived from Christ, who is our greatest gift.

Liturgy. The drama of the new covenant is enacted in ritual. Perhaps the greatest riches of Catholicism are to be found in the rites that surround the mystery of love. The use of symbols and artistic expression draws the human spirit through aesthetics to the realm of the sacred. It may well happen that with cultural change some of that symbolic wealth loses its meaning and needs to be reinterpreted or revitalized. New forms of expression better suited to particular people may give life to the message in more intelligible and acceptable ways. But we cannot do without ritual, because it is part of the myth. The story of the covenant of the heart is not simply a verbal declaration. Just as the prophets incarnated the first covenant in the language of poetry, and the priests gave it life in ritual, so too the new covenant is at home in the upper room, where the common elements of bread and wine enshrine the salvific act of the new era in a Passover setting.

Liturgy is the drama of religion. There the finest gifts of the human spirit come to the fore in ceremony, music, and art in a way that lifts the human spirit. The preached word is not a lecture or a lesson in catechism, but an appeal to the heart in setting forth the multifaceted story of salvation. The importance of all the features that go into liturgy can hardly be overstated. Music should draw on the best of the present without neglecting the inestimable legacy of the past. Architecture creates a mood and provides a setting, and much that is modern has enhanced our sense of the sacred. The "otherness" of God is reflected in the use of space, the presence of light, and the proximity of the worshipers to the sanctuary. Nothing is placed casually in a church; everything is a reminder that we stand on "sacred ground," where we encounter in a distinctive way the God of covenant who has made us his own. Why is it that our initial impressions of the cathedral of Chartres are never forgotten? In its symmetry and

breathtaking sweep heavenward it is a prayer in stone. Everything, even the finest detail, contributes to its beauty. The years
of human labor expended to make Chartres the lasting memorial
that it is say more about a living faith than do scholarly tomes.

Church Authority. The centrality of Christ in covenant theology
is nowhere more important than in the matter of authority. The
reason why scripture has long been seen as the eminent authority, even to the point of dividing Christianity, is because it so
clearly and unmistakably points to the person of Jesus and his
teaching. There is a real sense in which we all stand under the
judgment of the word, both church and believer, and thus the
scriptures will always retain a position of preeminence. Yet, as
the Second Vatican Council made clear, the scriptures do not
stand apart from the church. They were spawned by the church;
the New Testament was composed and approved within the
church as an expression of her belief. Since the church was in a
real sense the mother and "care giver" of the New Testament
library, as well as the authenticator of the Old Testament, she too
can authoritatively interpret the word of God. But once that is
said and done, it is clear that all in the church are subject to the
dictates of the scriptures.

Just as the word endows people within the church with a determined authority, so too it establishes the parameters. The New
Testament has a considerable amount to say about the use of
authority in the church, and history attests to the fact that it has
not always been faithfully observed. Officeholders in the church,
more than any others, must realize that it is a question of "Christ at
every turn." It is not they who are to be the centers of attention but
the Lord alone. As the ancient story goes, leaders in the church are
like so many fingers pointing to the moon. It is the moon that
counts, and it ill behooves any of us to get lost in the fingers.

The greater the authority, the greater the responsibility. If in
teaching, preaching, and sanctifying it is the living Christ that is
to the fore, by the same token it is also Christ who is alive and
present in those entrusted to our care. Nothing is to obscure the
relationship between Christ and his followers in any era. For this
reason authority in the New Testament is repeatedly called to be
self-effacing, the servant, the least of all. Authority stands at the

service of the covenanted people and never stands between Christ and his followers. This would only block the view, and that is unconscionable. We are well served if we return repeatedly to Paul's vision of leadership. It is in First Corinthians that we find his blueprint of church order. There were forms of "hero worship" in the Corinthian community, centering on Apollos, Kephas, and Paul. Paul will have none of it, as he reminds his hearers that none of their "heroes" had been crucified for them. The only role of leadership is service to the people, even when this means correction or admonition. For it is the leaders who "belong to you," not vice versa, just as "you [belong] to Christ, and Christ, to God" (1 Cor 3:22).

And so, there are more things involved in this covenant of the heart, "dear Horatio, than are dreamt of in your philosophy." As we go through the change that has become synonymous with flexibility and even courage, there are certain verities that must remain intact. There are changes in our understanding of the message of faith, and that is to be expected. A new generation is not simply a blueprint of the past. To live is to change, and to have lived long is to have changed much. But through it all it is this notion of a people covenanted with the living God in Christ Jesus that remains the constant. Few of us would embrace wholeheartedly the church of the Middle Ages. When we think of the crusades today, our moral awareness finds the waging of war a giant negative, and we stand rather incredulous before a belief that saw war waged in God's interest as an act of virtue. It was an era when Armageddon was already being played out on a field where good and evil were seen in terms of Christians and Muslims. Yes, there were people like Francis of Assisi who saw dialogue as much more salutary than bloodshed, but his was not the commonly held view. Saints preached the crusades and Louis of France, saint and king, contributed to his sainted image by limiting the number of prostitutes permitted to accompany the crusaders. This was a holy war, and God was clearly on the side of the crusaders. This notion continued into modern times as Christian countries locked in warfare prayed with equal fervor that their efforts be blessed by the God who upheld the righteous and defended the just. But the stark horror of modern warfare and the dangers inherent in its nuclear dimension have adjusted our moral sense on the whole question of war. One should add to that the deepening of our awareness of the "mind of Christ," which has also made a contribution.

Christian Unity. One of the quantum leaps of our times is the increased sense of unity that exists among Christians. This has nothing to do with the formal acceptance of agreements among the churches, although that too is an eventuality devoutly to be wished. We are here looking at the understanding that is taking place on the grass-roots level, and it is here that covenant theology has made a contribution. Regardless of the differences that divide Christians, many of which are proving to be solvable, the one baptism uniting all believers establishes the plateau for discussion. God's covenant with the baptized has led us to understand that Christ is operative not only in the personal lives of other Christians but in their churches as well, binding us together in God's Spirit under the headship of Christ. Our sense of community may not be complete, but it is real. We now begin with what unites us and work with added resolve to overcome differences. Our bonding with God has placed in new and bold relief our bonds with other Christians.

The covenant of the heart as seen by Jeremiah was not sterile or law centered; it moved away from simple external observance. The new covenant reaches deep inside the human person and fashions moral posture around love and gratitude. It does not disregard law and precept but refuses to make them paramount. Today much of the discord in doctrinal and moral conversation makes Christian faith almost totally issue oriented. Undoubtedly some of these issues are quite grave and merit attention, but this is not the heart of the religious experience. It is God's love for the world and the fact that a church is a people that has bonded with the living God that give meaning to everything we do. These must be the starting point and the focal point of all our conversation. If they do not emerge as the source of our greatest joy, then the enunciation of principle will be simply that. Unless Christianity tells the story and revels in the myth—just the way the gospels do, then as we try to move mountains, we shall never move hearts.

One of my students in a Catholic school of theology was preparing for the Presbyterian ministry. She was a lawyer, the mother of a family, and legally blind. She read only with the aid of a large magnifying glass. For years she had tackled incredible obstacles to reach her goal. In preaching class one day she was speaking on the cross and recounting particular experiences of suffering with which she was distantly acquainted. One of the Catholic seminarians in the class suggested that nothing could be more convincing than her own story, and it was that which should be recounted. Rather reluctantly she moved from a third-person narrative to a first. The point was well taken. Her own trials brought faith to life; she was her own best homily. It is the story that moves. We need but think of the unforgettable conclusion of Francois Poulenc's opera "Dialogues of the Carmelites," which portrays the martyrdom of a convent of Carmelite nuns during the French Revolution. At the opera's conclusion one nun after another moves toward the guillotine while chanting the "Salve Regina." The religious experience is stirring and profound. If it is a covenant of the heart that we are about, then we can never forget to tell the story.

GRACE AND DUTY

There is a delicate balance to be maintained between law and freedom, and neither Judaism nor Christianity has always been successful in maintaining it. When laws are seen as stepping-stones to holiness, then the covenanted life quickly becomes a matter of observance geared to safeguard one's eternal destiny. Even if not always maintained with unfailing success, law observance makes for a neat and tidy way of living; it offers clarity and a very specific goal. But it is above all a task to be performed. The words of the ritual for religious profession sum it up very clearly. In speaking of the rule and constitutions, the superior says: "And if you observe all these things, I promise you eternal life." It may well be that not too many religious succeed in this undertaking with maximum efficiency, but at least the goal is clear. This is a task to be pursued, a striving for perfection, a mountain climb to achieve eternal life.

In Jewish life the priority of the law can be seen in the plethora of precepts that went beyond the biblical law codes to embrace almost every facet of human existence. The Mishna, an extensive collection of Jewish laws, is a classic example of how Jewish life became encased in detailed prescriptions. It was precisely against this type of legal mindset that Jesus inveighed during his ministry. While the emphasis on law within the church has had its peaks and its valleys, the preconciliar church of the early twentieth century was a moment marked by strong emphasis on the law. Canon law touched every aspect of the Christian life. This translated into a strong legalism in various areas of church life. Religious life, for example, was governed by canon law in the way the life was to be lived, with local legislation determining in detail the way in which each day was to be spent. Invariably excessive emphasis on law drains the faith response of its basic vitality.

In this connection it is helpful to review the relationship between law and grace. As the present study has indicated, there are some critical questions raised about the original relationship between the Exodus and Sinai events. Nonetheless, as the biblical text comes to us, the Sinai experience is seen as Israel's response to the graciousness of Yahweh in liberating his people. The covenant is initiated by Yahweh himself as an expression of his will to make the people his own. While the covenant law stands at the heart of the bond (Ex 20–22), it is prefaced by the persuasive language of Yahweh's concern in bringing the people from the darkness of oppression in order to make them his own (Ex 19:3–6), and it concludes with repeated expressions of the people's willingness to bond with Yahweh (Ex 24:3–6). Law clearly finds its place within a context of grace. It is not a way of reaching God but the path to follow in responding to his experienced favor. The difference is substantial.

LOVE AS A GRACIOUS RESPONSE

In the great *Shema'* Deuteronomy summarizes the whole of the law in the commandment of love (Dt 6:4–9). Even in setting forth its body of laws (chaps. 12–26), it litanies first the acts of God's favor from Horeb (Sinai) to Canaan (chaps. 1–3). Moreover in the ceremony of covenant renewal at Shechem (Jos 24), it is on the basis of the favor and concern shown by Yahweh that the people are urged to abandon their service to false gods (vv. 5–13).

In the new covenant there is no less emphasis placed on divine favor than was the case in the former alliance. In fact, so strongly does Paul believe in the all-sufficient power of grace that he will admit of no competing factor in the process of salvation. The law as the avenue to justification proved totally inadequate. Good in itself, it was powerless to save and therefore finished by allying itself with sin and death. Rather than being a means of avoiding sin, it only enabled adherents to see their sin with greater clarity and to call it by name (Rom 7:7ff.). It is the goodness of God, which reaches us in Christ, that alone saves. It is not a question of law and grace for Paul; there is no "both/and" in the Christian life. If anything were to stand alongside faith on the path to salvation, it would rob Christ's redemptive outreach of its singular and total effectiveness. "By grace you have been saved by faith." This basic idea of salvation flowing from God's initiative, central to both Testaments, finds it fullest expression in Pauline teaching.[4]

All of this has clear pastoral implications. A covenant relationship must strive at every turn to uphold the primacy of love, especially as the need for legislation emerges. Before laws are made leadership must ask if the same end cannot be attained through exhortation or persuasion. Laws have a way of putting things neatly in place, but they also have a way of suffocating the human spirit. The marked emphasis on effective preaching today underscores the fact that it is Christian maturity through education and formation that best safeguards and channels covenant love.

Faith and Works. If for no other reason than to put an "old chestnut" to rest, it is well to state again that faith and works are not at odds. It is consoling to note that the conflict that raged around this issue in Reformation times has greatly subsided in modern times. If the biblical sequence of favor and law is kept in mind, then observance becomes a grateful response to God's saving action. Justification is not the end of a process but rather its beginning. Human nature in its weak and unaided condition can do nothing to merit God's favor anymore than it can succeed in observing a set of laws. One can only accept God's favor in faith. It is by believing that our inadequacy has been overcome in and through the generous act of Christ's self-donation and the appropriation of his victory in faith that grace is bestowed and sin overcome. It is in the light of this gift of God that we now hope to say "I have competed well; I have finished the race; I have kept the faith" (2 Tm 4:7). Law is subsequent to grace, not its competitor. The fact that God's love has made us holy, by no merit of our own, should evoke a response which ardently adheres to God's will. And it is at this point that the observance of the law, primarily the law of love, comes into play. Without this human response Christianity would be incomplete. There would be no bilateralism to the covenant at all. Grace and duty both have a place, but both must be viewed in perspective.

Christianity is not antinomian. Justification does not result in a free and unfettered spirit guided only by reason. As we have seen, Christ replaces the covenant law of the Old Testament. Therefore, the true disciple's response to God's favor centers on Jesus, who is mediator, priest, and victim. That being the case, the response to the covenant is determined by his life and teaching. We are called to have "that mind" in us that was also his. Therefore, the Christian conscience asks itself constantly: What would be the response of Christ to this situation? In my relationship to God, my neighbor, the covenant community as a whole, what is my ethical posture to be, based on the teaching of the gospel?[5]

The Sermon on the Mount. The difference between the terms of the two covenants, however, is central to our discussion. The way in which the Israelites fulfilled their responsibilities was carefully articulated. The law left little undefined. But this is not the way in which the new covenant is delineated. It is not an ethic of specific commandments. The decalogue, for example, only specifies the outer limits; it is not the apogee of Christian conduct, but rather the point of departure. If Christianity has a "magna carta," it is to be found in the sermon on the mount. It is the law of charity that is normative in the Christian life, and its significance is not exhausted in particular laws or precepts. It finds expression in countless ways and on many levels; it is not circumscribed but open-ended. Matthew 5–7 is not a new decalogue; rather, it sets forth a series of examples expressing the ways in which the love of God and neighbor comes to life. It does not exhaust the possibilities or say all that has to be said; it simply illustrates ways in which covenant response is channeled. Yet those very examples enunciate the principle of total self-giving that was at the heart of Christ's own mission. Christ remains, then, the sole measure of what discipleship means. The many examples of Christ—his outreach to the needy, compassion for the widow of Naim, forgiveness of the adulteress, willingness to visit the house of Zacchaeus, pardon from the cross—are illustrative of the ways in which new covenant love expresses itself. In washing the feet of his disciples, Jesus gives meaning to a lowly spirit. When it comes to leadership in the Christian community, there are no levitical laws or detailed rubrics, no blueprints outlining duties or obligations. But there is the repeated reminder that those who are first must be the least and those in authority must be the servants of all. In other words, few things are said of a detailed or specific nature, but the radical and far-reaching character of what is taught reaches the very core of our being. When one is called to love without counting the cost, the horizons are unlimited.

Pastoral Implications. It is often said that a homily should make a very clear moral point. That there is wisdom here is amply borne out by the rambling character of some preaching, which leaves both the speaker and the congregation at sea. Homilies generally do point out ways in which the Christian life is to be lived. Yet a message centering on what God has done and continues to do for us, one more didactic than exhortatory, is quite appropriate at times, when it stokes the fires of gratitude and allows the listener to make his or her own application.

This way of looking at the Christian life has countless ramifications. Those of us who lived through an earlier day in the church's life realize that authority found it much easier to rule by edict than persuasion. Notices on the bulletin board were the accepted way of having one's will executed, whether in seminaries, religious houses, or college dorms. There was little attempt to let "sweet reason" win the day through dialogue and persuasion.

Yet Christ taught by his life, his example, and by his exhortations. While no one can duplicate the life of the gospel Jesus,

117

countless people in the course of history have lived out in their own time and circumstances the moral posture of the Master. The fact that we are not asked to make the total sacrifice that marked Jesus' life cannot reduce our call to a life of generosity and selflessness, in our limited circumstances, patterned on the example of the Lord.

In light of the gratuity of salvation, the question naturally arises as to the place *merit* holds in this discussion. Catholicism's long-held position became a major factor in the Protestant-Catholic controversy of the sixteenth century. The Lutheran rejection of indulgences did not rest solely on their allegedly being sold but rather in seeing them as a means of attaining salvation. Anything that gave the appearance of being "earned" was seen by the Reformers as being at odds with the singular beneficence of God's saving action.

Undergirding the Catholic position was the idea of a temporal punishment for sin, a need for atonement for sins already remitted. These relics of sin could be atoned for in an interim state after death, known as purgatory, or on this side of the grave, through the performance of salutary acts or good deeds. The controversy became particularly heated when indulgences were granted in connection with monetary offerings, even though it was the total issue around which the tempest swirled.

From the Catholic perspective atonement for sin is an integral part of faith. Authentic sorrow is accompanied by an honest desire to make amends, which finds expression in penance, charity, and other good works. Just as faith comes to life in love, so too forgiveness seeks to express gratitude in voluntary expressions of mortification or self-denial. A major difficulty arises, however, when atonement is measured in terms of days, months, or years. As well intentioned as such a system of credits and debits may have been, it lent itself to a mindset that could barter its way to total reconciliation.

In a former day indulgences were much more common. It may well be that this general decline in the recourse to indulgences was influenced by the theological insight provided by modern studies on the meaning of *metanoia*. Conversion is part of the salvific process, God intended and God directed, transpiring under the action of his grace. It signifies both a disengagement and engagement, a turning around on the road, leaving behind a past of sin and "flesh" and redirecting our lives toward a fuller engagement in Christ through the action of the Spirit. Good deeds are not an acquisition or a means of obtaining favor; rather, they flow inherently from one's newfound life in God. As Paul VI stated in "Paenitemini," the most important document on this topic in modern times, conversion expresses itself in prayer, fasting, and monetary contributions, but even more specifically in outreach to the poor.[6]

This carries us back once more to our initial thesis. If the new covenant has any meaning it is this: salvation is not some end-time reality we strive to achieve; it is something already possessed, albeit in its initial phase, and any expression of salutary works is simply an expression of this new inner force, eternal life already at work, expressing itself in gratitude for a justification already conferred. This does not make Christian activity or traditional expressions of penance and charity any less significant. But it does mean that we approach them with a totally different perspective.

Dear Lord, teach me to love. Teach me to love you and my neighbor as the greatest good in my life. Your love for me is already present in countless ways. But nothing is worse than ingratitude; I want my life to be an expression of thanks. Besides the many good things of this life that you have given me, I am grateful for the covenant of the heart, for new life in you, for the new family, the new home, and the new destiny. I am so undeserving. Help me to show my love by making your will my own and then bringing it to life in the world. Amen.

FOR STUDY AND DISCUSSION

1. Discuss the role of the arts in telling the Christian story.
2. Discuss the importance of creeds and definitions and their relationship to the story.
3. Discuss division and polarization in the church and their impact on the credibility of the message.
4. Liturgy is spoken of as the drama of religion. Does that match your experience?

5. What do you see as the role of leadership and authority in the church?
6. Are we still growing in our understanding of God's message? Does the message itself continue to unfold?
7. How can we keep the balance between law and the primacy of love?
8. Catholic and Protestant polemics often centered on the relationship between law and good works. How do you see that question today?
9. What is your understanding of merit, indulgences, and temporal punishment due to sin?
10. Why is the sermon on the mount central to any consideration of Christian ethics?

COVENANT REDEMPTION

Therefore, since we have a great high priest who has passed through the heavens, Jesus, the Son of God, let us hold fast to our confession. For we do not have a high priest who is unable to sympathize with our weaknesses, but one who has similarly been tested in every way, yet without sin. So let us confidently approach the throne of grace to receive mercy and to find grace for timely help. (Heb 4:14–16)

The Redeemed Redeemer. In Richard Wagner's monumental music drama *Parsifal,* knights guard and draw nourishment from the Grail, the cup used by Christ at the Last Supper. Yet the atmosphere of their domain is somber and overcast. The suffering Amfortas presides over the Grail as he bears a wound that will not heal, the retribution for a past transgression. The seductress Kundry, who once mocked Christ on the cross, stands condemned and wanders aimlessly in search of redemption. The attendant knights, because of Amfortas's unwillingness to uncover the life-giving Grail, age constantly. In the third act the young and innocent Parsifal arrives in the hall of the Grail on Good Friday morning. To Amfortas he brings healing; to Kundry, baptism and forgiveness; to the knights, renewed life in his uncovering the Grail. His action is redemptive. In the final moments of the opera he holds the sacred cup aloft before the worshiping knights. And from above a choir of heavenly voices sings with eloquent and touching beauty: "Höchsten Heiles Wunder! Erlösung dem Erlöser" ("This is the greatest miracle of all. Redemption has come to the Redeemer").

The meaning of this concluding apotheosis, like many features of this work, has been widely discussed and analyzed.[1] How is the Redeemer redeemed? The figure of Parsifal, as derived from medieval legend, is a Christian hero, and Wagner has laden his music drama with Christian symbols. Even more than that, Parsifal is a Christ figure, who in his innocence and genuine altruism brings salvation to others. But this he does only when he himself has experienced the pain that accompanies redemption, when he has grown through personal sacrifice, when he has shown compassion to the suffering Amfortas and Kundry, and when he has rejected the tempting wiles of sin presented by Klingsor, the bewitching sorcerer. So, in order to bring redemption the redeemer had first to be redeemed.

The Christianity of the nineteenth century had lost much of its effectiveness. Wagner's ambivalent feelings about the church can be at least partially explained by its culturally overladen and encrusted state. Teachings, doctrines, and ceremonies were the visible remnants of the great myth, which Wagner felt had an overwhelming transforming power. Therefore, it may well have been from all of this that the Redeemer had to be redeemed.

Yet in our study of the covenant this question may be raised: Is there a sense in which the mediator himself must receive the benefits of mediation? Is there a Christian sense in which the Redeemer must himself be redeemed? The answer, it would seem, lies in the fact that Christ is in the new covenant both priest and victim. He not only suffers *for,* but he suffers *with.* Christian tradition is unanimous in the conviction that Christ is not redeemed from a state of sin. But is there a deliverance apart from sinfulness that is proper to his human state?

The reply to the above is affirmative when we see redemption as a transition from death to life, from mortality to immortality, from flesh to spirit. It is the Jesus of the gospels who says: "There is a baptism with which I must be baptized, and how great is my anguish until it is accomplished" (Lk 12:50). And to the disciples: "Can you...be baptized with the baptism with which I am baptized" (Mk 10:38)? The baptism to which he refers is not liberation from sin but rather his death-resurrection, which will effect in him that transformation from flesh to Spirit that is the prototype of the Christian sacrament. If he who did not know sin became sin for us (2 Cor 5:21), then there is a sense in which the

Redeemer is redeemed. He took upon himself all the effects of sin, was delivered up, and finally was rescued by the Father.

Priest and People. Therefore, the mediator of the new covenant is not the detached and lofty high priest of the old. In being fully identified with his people, he is fully sympathetic to their suffering and pain. As both priest and victim he establishes a new covenant in his own blood, thus conferring on this bond an inestimable and perpetual value. It was in the days of his "flesh" that "he offered prayers and supplications with loud cries and tears to the one who was able to save him from death" (Heb 5:7). Christ, too, prayed for deliverance and in the Father's response was "redeemed."

This gives to covenant a dimension of singularity and distinctiveness. It moves away from a rigid legal framework and emphasizes strongly the notion of God's concern and identification with the covenanted people. In short, the God of the covenant stands very much with the people he makes his own. Ours is not a priest detached from victimhood but rather one who attained our freedom at a very dear price. He is the priest who experiences redemption with us. Christian holiness springs from a realization and appreciation of this fact.

"CALLED TO BE HOLY" (ROM 1:7)

In Hebrew thought Yahweh was both the prototype and the cause of holiness (Lv 22:31f.). The word carries the sense of "otherness," something separated from daily experience, belonging to another sphere of existence. With the profane signifying the common or the everyday, the holy stood at the other end of the spectrum. As close as Yahweh might come to his people, he was still not one of them; in fact, the scriptures repeatedly assert that no one could look upon him and live. To speak of Yahweh was to speak only an approximation. The term "holiness" pointed to an eternal, overarching God who consistently upholds justice but is inherently related to another realm of existence.[2]

The human person was holy to the extent that he or she reflected that "otherness" of Yahweh. Holiness was to make God present within the community. Since the law was the expression of Yahweh's will for his people, then it had to reflect the values central to his own existence. Therefore, to live the law and observe "his precepts and statutes" was not only an act of submission but a visible incarnation of the otherness of the invisible God. This was what made the holy person different as a representative of transcendent values. A holy people separated themselves from the tides of social change, from the norms of human conduct at odds with the ways of God, from that neutral way of being based on the accepted reality, a pragmatic spirit, or personal convenience.

Holiness in antiquity also went beyond moral conduct. The "unholy" covered a plethora of things seen to be at odds with divine integrity. Decay in any form, not only sin, was abhorrent, including skin disorders, blood discharges, molds, and funguses. Such abnormalities were at odds with completeness and integrity; in Hebrew thought holiness and wholeness were very much related.

In its origins, then, law was anything but a burden. A gift to Israel, it was the centerpiece of the covenant relationship. It was never intended as a burden or an insupportable weight; it was an unmerited insight into the mind of God, giving a clear and unobstructed view of how life was to be lived and "otherness" made proximate.

With the new covenant all of this is simply transposed into another key. The underlying objective remains the same: the holiness of the believer brought about by a new relationship to God. The difference is that Christ substitutes for the law. It is not conformity with a set of laws that effects sanctity but rather faith in Christ, who evokes a faith-filled moral response.

Atonement. Any discussion of covenant holiness soon centers upon atonement for sin. The past must be put behind us and unresolved indebtedness addressed. In the Old Testament this was done through sacrificial blood rites executed by the priests (Lv 4:4), or, as Hebrews will later state it, "without the shedding of blood there is no forgiveness" (9:22). In the new dispensation this is the work of Christ alone, the sole high priest, who enters the holy place only once to make an all-inclusive atonement. This is done through his atoning death, which in Hebrews, as we have seen, is presented in liturgical terms. The hues of the contrast are sharp indeed; the past is but a weak shadow of what Christ has accomplished. In making the "will" of the Father his own, he lifts the weight of our sins in a once-and-for-all offering in the heavenly sanctuary.[3]

Holiness, then, finds its beginning in sin or at least the recognition of the alienation that sin confers. This is to use *sin* in its broadest sense; it represents the forces of this world, the power of evil, all that is at variance with the otherness of God. Before embarking on a new life in God, or better, a new life in Christ, there must be an atoning death to sin and its consequences rooted in the reception of baptism. Only then does one set out on the new road of sanctity.[4]

Conversion. In a very few words this is the meaning of *metanoia* or biblical conversion, a disengagement from sin and an engagement with God that is ongoing and incremental. It is not to be equated with an unsullied record or the absence of any stumbling along the way. What comes to the fore is a change in vision, a different perspective, a fundamental redirecting of our spiritual energies. To speak of conversion as ongoing means that it is not a fait accompli; it is in motion and looks to growth.

Yet as we have seen in the whole biblical chronology of the "now" and the "not yet," while conversion looks to a future terminal point, it has a finality in the present as well. Just as the single act of Christ's atonement will never be repeated, so too the baptismal incorporation into Christ has a once-and-for-all character as well (Rom 6:10f.). Once a person has been brought to life from death, that person does not revert to a life that spells death once again. It is for this reason that we have difficulty in reconciling Pauline teaching with a theology of sin remission that carries the serious sinner back and forth between sin and grace. What must be said in favor of the "fundamental option" is its ability to weigh moral conduct in the light of a basic direction or goal to which the believer may remain attached even in failure and from which he or she may definitively separate through a pattern of moral indifference or rejection.[5]

And yet conversion is only a beginning; holiness does not rest solely on forgiveness received. In speaking of our newly acquired access to the inner sanctuary with Christ, our high priest, the author of Hebrews wants to contrast the new and old eras. Whereas formerly access to the most holy place was permitted once a year to the high priest alone, now the new people of God stands as a body within the heavenly court.

What is clearly at the heart of this imagery of Hebrews—and so pivotal in the writings of John and Paul—is a direct and immediate access to God. The sanctuary imagery depicts what Paul expresses in the family or household of God. It is not that we are bound to God by choice or, much less, through law observance. It is the shared life with God, the gift of the Spirit conferred by the risen Christ, that results in the "indwelling" of the Trinity within us. No access to God could be more personal or unfettered, conditioned by neither time nor place, neither circumstance nor observance. We no longer worship God in Jerusalem or on Mount Gerizim; ours is a worship in Spirit and truth (Jn 4:20–24).

Holiness, then, is nothing more than awareness of this new reality of our life. Our "otherness" consists in our being members of the household of God and seeing that our choices in life are reflective of the trinitarian family to which we belong. A few verses from Romans 8 summarize it succinctly:

> *For those who are led by the Spirit of God are children of God. For you did not receive a spirit of slavery to fall back into fear, but you received a spirit of adoption, through which we cry, "Abba, Father!" The Spirit itself bears witness with our spirit that we are children of God, and if children, then heirs, heirs of God and joint heirs with Christ, if only we suffer with him so that we may also be glorified with him. (Rom 8:14–17)*

To be children of the new covenant is to live with the Father, who sent his Son out of love; it is to live with the Son, who, in making the Father's will his own, has been raised up, endowed with a new life-giving force; it is to live with the Spirit, who is the pulsating life of the risen Christ, now shared with all believers. Our access to the heavenly sanctuary translates into being members of the family of God, enabling us to call God Father with the endearment proper to Christ himself. Herein lies the heart of Christian holiness.

Ongoing Transformation. Neither the former nor the present covenant sees holiness as a static state. In the relevant passages from Second Corinthians, which we have discussed, Paul speaks very clearly of an ongoing transformation. The veil worn by Moses masked a continually fading glory, while we, with no veil separating us from the glory of Christ, are being drawn to him ever more forcefully (2 Cor 3:18). Yet what does this transformation actually mean? To know God is to know Christ, who is the way, the truth, and the life (Jn 14:5–10). Therefore, growth in holiness has to mean growth in our knowledge and love of Christ. Prayer must be Christ-centered; spirituality must drink deep of the gospel. The patristic dictum has lost none of its force: "To be ignorant of the scriptures is to be ignorant of Christ." If to know Jesus is to know God, then our principal source of knowledge has to be the word of God. Meditation may mean many things for many people, but one of its nonnegotiables is a prayerful reading of the gospels in discerning the teaching and comportment of Jesus. How else do we know how to react to the countless problems that beset us? How do we make our choices? What is written is written for our instruction. How are we to view violence? hatred? lust? greed? The answer is found in the sermon on the mount (Mt 5–7). What are the limits of our forgiveness? The answer is startlingly clear in the story of the lost son (Lk 15): there are no limits. Is that not the meaning of forgiving "not seven times but seventy times seven times" (Mt 18:22)? As we read the gospels, time after time the comportment of Jesus steps away from the conventional wisdom and breaks new ground. We see the Jesus open to all, the one seeking the sinner and the rejected, the one who not only taught humility but exemplified it in washing his disciples' feet. It is this that fashions our responses as Christians. These are the terms of the covenant as taught and, more important, lived by him who is priest and victim of the new dispensation.

This remains an open-ended response. There is no question of parameters or limits. What the Jesus of the gospels sets forth is not a blueprint but examples. We may never experience the same set of circumstances envisioned in the gospel presentation, yet the basic response remains unaltered. It is in applying the evangelical teaching to our daily life that growth in the covenant relationship, the passage from "glory to glory," becomes clear. No sooner do we say "it is done" than we realize that it is hardly enough. As we move more and more toward "the Good," the influence of "the flesh" or the former person diminishes. Our perspectives broaden; our Christian life intensifies; we feel ourselves in less danger for having cast our lot with the Lord, "our portion and our cup."

God and Neighbor. John reminds us that we cannot love God, whom we do not see, if we do not love our neighbor, whom we do see. This illustrates the two-pronged central teaching of Jesus in the great commandment: love of God and neighbor is inseparable. It is the covenant of God with a *people* that places this teaching in sharp relief. And much as God's personal care touches us and as much as the scriptures say about our individual response, it is always as part of a community, a church, a people that we are saved. This has important consequences for the way our life is lived; it forces us to see that response to the needs of our neighbor is integral to our covenant relationship with God. The meaning of the body of Christ, the household of God, the garden of God—all biblical images touching on our divine relationship—springs ultimately from the fact that God has bonded with a people. Our work with soup kitchens, after-school programs, house construction for the poor, AIDS sufferers, minority rights—all expressions of social awareness—is tied in with our covenant faith.

We worship together because of the public and communal nature of our commitment. The same bonds that link us to God link us with one another. The liturgical and sacramental life of the church intensifies our growth in God but also our sense of outreach to one another, especially the neediest. We can only be grateful for the extent to which the revised liturgy has heightened our awareness of community as well as diversity in ministry.[6]

A community needs direction and leadership. Christ has provided this as well. We remain sensitive to those who are teachers in the covenant community. We adhere to their teaching as the will of Christ, just as we ask them to be open to new ways and directions stirring within the church. If authority is called to serve—and there is no clearer teaching in the New Testament—then those who exercise leadership must remain sensitive to the views of those whom they serve.

Above all, the covenant community must avoid splintering or polarization. Harsh and strident voices can never succeed in reflecting the image of the humble Christ. It is undeniable that the division of the Eastern and Western churches dating from the close of the first millennium and the later major division of the Western church itself weigh heavily on us. Our fractured covenant community has never recovered from its fall; we can never remain complacent. Recent steps toward unity since Vatican II have been encouraging but not overwhelmingly so. We see the obstacles that seem to loom large on the horizon instead of all that unites us. That clear call of the Johannine Jesus to unity has to resonate deeply within us—and the actual separation deeply pain us—if we are not to settle for the status quo. It is all part of covenant commitment.

"Called to Be Holy." We are called to be saints, a short phrase that says a great deal. It is our vocation, something to which all of us are called. The meaning of the Greek word for church (*ekklesia*) and its Hebrew antecedent (*qahal*) says nothing about free association or assembly for a common goal. It says everything about God's plan and God's initiative. The word *call* or *vocation* is at the heart of both verbal roots. We are where we are because God wants us there. He has called us out of darkness into his own wondrous light. We have no claim, no merit, no title. We are simply wanted, and it has led to this wondrous community where God's favor and power meet us at every turn. We have bonded with God because he initiated the bond.

We are all called to holiness. This point was sounded strongly at Vatican II but not too well established prior to that. It is inspiring to witness a canonization, to hear the applause as someone is raised in St. Peter's to the "glory of Bernini." This is the church's "Hall of Fame." We all have need of role models. But the fact is that holiness is to be normative in the Christian life. We are all saints, if we live in God's grace in the here and now a life that is to perdure into the life beyond. The more each of us realizes what that calling means, the brighter will be the light shining in the darkness and more savored the salt giving flavor to life.

In Memory of Me

The angelic voices acknowledge Parsifal as the "redeemed Redeemer" as he holds the cup of the Grail before the kneeling knights. It is a moment with clear eucharistic allusions, and if we go behind the legend, we are reminded of the clear redemptive features of the symbolic act of Jesus at the Last Supper. The eucharist is first of all a memorial of his death. For as often as we eat this bread and drink this cup, we "proclaim the death of the Lord until he comes" (1 Cor 11:26). The passage from death to life was Jesus' "baptism," a transition that effected his "redemption." The eucharist replays that event in sacred sign. But that death was also a defining moment for all humankind. The debt was canceled; the handwriting that was against us was removed; access to the heavenly sanctuary was made available to all. We are once more at one with God. The gaping wound of Amfortas is healed by the touch of Parsifal's spear. Redemption is achieved, and eucharist memorializes that defining moment of which we are all the beneficiaries.

It is safe to say that nowhere in the Christian life is the meaning of covenant more clearly highlighted than in the eucharist. In the synoptics' Last Supper narrative Jesus links the two covenants in echoing Moses' words at Sinai: "This is the blood of the covenant" (Ex 24:8). The text is altered only to underscore fulfillment: "*my* blood" (Mt 26:28; Mk 14:24); "the *new* covenant" (Lk 22:20; 1 Cor 11:25). This blending of two eras makes for an enduring covenant continuum from Sinai and the upper room to the present day. In every mass the church *re*presents and *re*enacts the offering of Jesus and through him brings us back to Sinai itself, where God and people were initially joined. For this reason the eucharist is the apogee of the church's life, the summit of worship, the moment in which God and his people are most at one. As the redeemed Redeemer, Christ reaches out to God and humanity, a posture perfectly summarized in eucharist where he is both priest and victim.

On Sinai, Moses took the blood of the animal victims, held it aloft, and sprinkled it on the altar and the people in forming the solemn bond. For the ancients, life and blood were one, indeed life was in the blood; loss of blood meant the loss of life. This gave blood a sacred character as a life force, and it was on this basis that it became part of ritual. Life was tied into the meal as well; sharing a meal with another was to wish that person well in terms that were rich in symbolism. To break bread with an enemy was an inherent contradiction, a serious profaning of the sacred. In transposing the melody to a cultic key, to eat a sacrifice that had been offered to God and now belonged to the realm of the holy presumed proper dispositions and connoted a wholly distinctive relationship with the deity. Following the blood rites in Exodus, Moses and his companions ate of the sacrificial meal (Ex 24:11). As an important part of the weave, the Jesus of the synoptic gospels memorializes the new covenant in the context of a meal with his disciples. This is done in a Passover setting with sacrificial blood. All the elements of the original covenant are present: the mediator, the victim, the sacrifice, and the meal.

But covenant carries the eucharist to another level of understanding: the sense of community. In this study community has emerged repeatedly, because it is inextricably linked with biblical covenant. As a church we have never lost sight of this link between eucharist and community; it is strongly in evidence in the postconciliar age, a helpful antidote to the privatization of religion so prevalent today. It is sufficient to note that even in a bygone era, with a somewhat time-worn theology, there was never such a thing as a "private" mass. Even though a priest celebrated mass alone, the act was by nature public, an offering of the Christian community. Certainly today that public, or better, ecclesial, character of the eucharist is much to the fore. The more passive and silent presence of earlier times has given way to an active participation through which the congregation can more clearly give expression to its role as covenant maker. In architecture the configuration of sacred space has resulted in a stronger sense of the people's close connection with the altar and their unity among themselves. This has been heightened by the variety of ministries within the eucharist so much in evidence at every Sunday liturgy. The ongoing discussion about the position of the priest at the altar is not unrelated to the covenant theme. With the priest-presider facing the people, the dialogic relationship between community and celebrant is placed in strong relief. The preconciliar liturgy, in which priest and people stood together vis-à-vis the altar, underscored the solidarity of the entire community (priest and people) as co-offerers and covenant makers with God (the altar) the sole correspondent.

It is within the eucharist that the community gives expression to its ongoing concerns. It has long been seen as the church's most efficacious prayer, with worship given to God through the mediation of his Son, who is both priest and victim. In the efficacy of Jesus' prayer there is compensation for our mortal weakness. It is here that we best express sorrow for our transgressions, realizing that atonement is one of the first fruits of the covenant. The limitless benefits of redemption make people of every generation its beneficiaries, and it is in eucharist that this strikingly comes to life. It is here that our requests are vocalized, especially our thanks to God, the meaning of eucharist. Thanksgiving and gratitude pass from eucharist to daily life in upright and grace-filled personal conduct.

The community dimension of the eucharist serves as a springboard for living out the social agenda of the church.[7] The covenant community is one sent to be the leaven of society, bringing justice to the wronged, effecting peace among the unreconciled, and serving the needs of the poor. The unity of all believers around the table of the Lord without distinction typifies the all-embracing spirit of the Christian life. There is no protocol of priority or privilege as we approach the communion table. The word of God proclaimed solemnly Sunday after Sunday is a constant summons to live in a spirit of concern for others. To realize that the full impact of the century-old social doctrine of the church has not been grasped by the Christian community as a whole only points up our need for greater awareness. The church is not a detached onlooker with its gaze fixed on a world beyond; it is an active player on the historical and sociopolitical scene. Human choices, in countless instances, have a moral component, and it is there that the individual Christian, as well as the church, has a responsibility to speak and act. The covenant community has people with specific competencies whose task is to infuse the Christian component into the human endeavor wherever it is appropriate. Unfortunately, this can be interpreted as a narrow sectarianism desirous of imposing its own religious agenda. If that is the case, then we want nothing of it. But the fact is that Christianity is a humanizing faith engaged in promoting "whatever is just, whatever is pure, whatever is lovely, whatever is gracious" (Phil 4:8).

In the covenant with Noah, Yahweh reached beyond the human partners to the covenant to touch the whole of creation. The New Testament points to Christ as not only head of the church but the firstborn of all creation (Col 1:15–20). It is this dimension of Christian truth that sees the environment as sacred, to be preserved from wanton disregard and destruction. It is because the covenant embraces the whole of the world that surrounds us that those daily reminders of our responsibilities toward the planet take on added meaning. And in the eucharist the elements of bread and wine, products of the earth and human hands transformed into sacred priest and victim, become clear indications of the ties that join the Christian community to the world as a whole.

As a covenant of the heart, then, the eucharist binds us with the Lord in a sacramental repast of body and blood. It is the God of the covenant who provides nourishment for the human journey; it is he as well who is the lasting pledge of eternal life. When we speak of fulfillment in any terms, we are forced to ask whether Jeremiah's covenant of the heart could have been realized in any stronger way. In the eucharist God has written indelibly on the human heart the testimony of his love and concern. It is the Spirit who guides and directs our faith response. The mass intensifies that family life in God that comes to the disciple in baptism; if it is communal, it is also deeply personal. Those two features are integral to the meaning of the new covenant.

Centuries of art and music point up the aesthetics connected with eucharist. The eucharist is drama and myth par excellence. The mass has the inherent power to lift and ennoble the human spirit; it speaks to the best in all of us about personal worth. It is that affective, touching, even emotional dimension that is all too casually lost sight of. The reform of the liturgy brought clarity and understanding and at its best is unquestionably an aid to prayer. But it was never meant to leave behind the cultural legacy of a millennium and a half. It is hard to forget the absence of suitable music in the years after the council, fortunately alleviated by hymns from the classical Protestant tradition. In more recent years the situation has improved considerably. The role of the choir is reemerging to restore that important musical heritage that, no less than the cathedral at Chartres, is geared to lift the heart to those things "which are above."

This may give us some idea of why some people remain so attached to mass in Latin. This writer has not offered mass in Latin for nearly thirty years and is moved by no nostalgic feeling to do so. But sensitivity has improved. We very easily labeled people who loved the past as traditionalists and conservatives, people who had lost vision and could not move ahead. This may well have been the case. Yet it cannot be denied that others found in the former liturgy a relationship to the holy, a sense of mystery and "otherness," of quiet and peace, all of which is part of the drama. We all remember the stock answer to people who championed Latin in the liturgy: "But you can't understand it!" Such is a rather broad statement. But, even so, intelligibility is not the be-all and end-all of worship. The intellect plays an important part in faith, but it does not exhaust its meaning. The drama or the myth reaches us on another, more intuitive level, more strongly related to aesthetics than we often think; it is a dimension that is not to be casually discarded. The reformed liturgy has much to commend it, but the burning question remains: Do we lend the time and the effort, as presiders, as ministers, cantors, and choir, to make it a true experience of a bonded people with a living God?

There are many threads woven into the fabric of covenant. They have their origins in times and cultures distant from our own. As this work has tried to illustrate, there have been moments in our sacred history when these threads converged and intertwined to form a new design. Disparate colors found a unity in this tapestry centering ultimately on Christ the Lord. And the story continues to unfold. A bond connected with the Sinai peninsula some three thousand years ago continues to have implications for citizens of the world at the beginning of a new millennium. Christian belief sees the Sinai covenant as intensified and transposed to a new key in the saving work of God's Son, actualized in that mystery we term church. It is a story that embraces the world, people of every race and nation, without distinction of gender or social category. "There is neither Jew nor Greek, there is neither slave nor free person, there is not male and female" (Gal 3:28). "I will take you as my own people, and you shall have me as your God" (Ex 6:7). These words gave meaning to a sacred history long before Christ, and they have been enriched by what has transpired "in these last days." It is a wondrous story that will always merit the telling.

Lord Redeemer, firstborn of the redeemed, when I feel alone and disconsolate, help me to realize your covenant love. As isolated as I may feel, I am always part of a faith community. The covenant tells me of your personal love for me and for all my brothers and sisters in the church and beyond. Help me and all Christians to appreciate our responsibility toward the world and its citizens. In the hardships of my life, I am never alone. I am never abandoned. I am redeemed and am assured a wondrous future. Teach me to realize that I could never ask for more. In Jesus' name I pray. Amen.

FOR STUDY AND DISCUSSION

1. In what sense can we speak of Christ as the redeemed Redeemer?
2. What are the pastoral implications of Christ's close identification with his people?
3. Holiness as "otherness"—how does that differ from our common understanding?
4. Conversion of life is an ongoing state. Do I feel that sense of growth or do I settle for the status quo?
5. Salvation comes to us as members of a covenanted people. Is my idea of salvation too personal and detached?
6. What priority should ecumenism have for a covenanted people?
7. Discuss the eucharist as a summary of our covenanted life.

NOTES

Chapter 1

1. Walter Eichrodt, *Theology of the Old Testament* (Philadelphia: Westminster Press, 1967). For a popular yet scholarly overview of the covenant issue, see Delbert Hillers, *Covenant: The History of a Biblical Idea* (Baltimore: Johns Hopkins Press, 1969).

2. For a comprehensive treatment of the word and its significance, see Colin Brown, ed., *The New International Dictionary of Old Testament Theology*, "Covenant" (vol. 1) (Grand Rapids: Zondervan Publishing House, 1971).

3. Gerhard von Rad, *The Problem of the Hexateuch and Other Essays* (New York: McGraw-Hill, 1966), 1–78.

4. Martin Noth, *The History of Israel* (New York: Harper, 1960).

5. For varying views of the Sinai-Exodus question, see Roland de Vaux, *Early History of Israel* (London: Darton, Longman, & Todd, 1978), 401–19; Norman Gottwald, *The Tribes of Israel* (Maryknoll, N.Y.: Orbis Books, 1979).

6. Austin Flannery, ed., *Vatican Council II*, "Decree on Ecumenism," chap. 2, par. 11 (Northport, N.Y.: Costello Publishing Co., 1992).

7. George Mendenhall, *Law and Covenant in the Ancient Near East* (Pittsburgh: University of Pittsburgh Press, 1955).

8. Dennis McCarthy, *Treaty and Covenant* (Rome: Biblical Institute Press, 1981). McCarthy differs from Mendenhall in claiming the absence of the influence of the treaty form on the earliest stages of the Sinai tradition and the final redaction of Exodus 19–24. See also Dennis McCarthy, *Old Testament Covenant* (Richmond: John Knox Press, 1972).

9. Roland de Vaux, *Ancient Israel* (New York: McGraw-Hill, 1961), 484–93.

10. G. J. Botterweck and H. Ringren, eds., *Theological Dictionary of the Old Testament,* "Hesed" (vol. 5) (Grand Rapids: Eerdmans, 1974); Roderick MacKenzie, *Faith and History in the Old Testament* (Minneapolis: University of Minnesota Press, 1963), 32–45.

Chapter 2

1. This distinction was introduced by Albrect Alt, *Essays on Old Testament History and Religion* (Sheffield: JSOT Press, 1989).

2. For a treatment of covenant law and its relationship to qualities in Yahweh and the community, see John McKenzie, "Aspects of Old Testament Thought," *New Jerome Biblical Commentary* (New Jersey: Prentice Hall, 1990), 1298–1301.

3. For a literary and form critical study of the decalogue in context, see Eduard Nielsen, *The Ten Commendments in New Perspective* (Naperville, Ill.: A. R. Allenson, 1968).

4. On law and the Christian life, see Charles H. Dodd, *Gospel and Law* (New York: Columbia University Press, 1951).

Chapter 3

1. On the Abrahamitic and Noaitic covenants, see Bruce Vawter, *On Genesis* (New York: Doubleday, 1977) 134–37, 203–25. Also Walter Brueggemann, *Genesis* (Atlanta: John Knox Press, 1982); Claus Westermann, *Genesis* (Minneapolis: Augsburg Publishing House, 1986).

2. For the covenant imprint on the human creation narrative, see Luis Alonso-Schoekel, "Sapiential and Covenant Themes in Genesis 2–3," *Theology Digest* (1965), 3–10.

3. On the redaction and theology of the Colossians hymn, see Bruce Vawter, *CBQ* 33 (1971), 62–81; Ernst Käsemann, *Essays on New Testament Themes* (Naperville, Ill.: A. R. Allanson, 1964).

4. George E. Wright, *Shechem, the Biography of a Biblical City* (New York: McGraw-Hill, 1965); Gottwald, *The Tribes of Israel.* For questions of structure and interpretation, see W. T. Koopmans, *Joshua and Poetic Narrative* (Sheffield: JSOT Press, 1990).

5. On the Shechem covenant form, see Dennis McCarthy, *Old Testament Covenant* (Richmond: John Knox Press, 1972).

6. Hillers sees the Davidic covenant, as well as the covenants with Noah and Abraham, as strictly unilateral. I see elements of bilateralism in the covenant with David and Abraham, while admitting the strong emphasis on divine initiative. See Hillers, *Covenant*, chap. 5.

7. On the new covenant, see Bruce Vawter, *The Conscience of Israel* (New York: Sheed and Ward, 1961), 271–77; John Bright, *Jeremiah* (Garden City: Doubleday, 1965), 269–88. Also see Harold H. Rowley, *The Faith of Israel* (London: SCM Press, 1956); Lawrence Boadt, *Jeremiah 26–52* (Wilmington: Michael Glazier, 1982).

Chapter 4

1. For a succinct presentation of contemporary exegetical thought on the Last Supper, see David N. Freedman, ed., *The Anchor Bible Dictionary*, "The Last Supper" (vol. 4) (Garden City: Doubleday, 1992), 234–40.

2. For a classical if somewhat dated study of the Last Supper narratives, see Joachim Jeremias, *The Eucharistic Words of Jesus* (Philadelphia: Fortress Press, 1977).

3. For literary and historical questions surrounding the Jerusalem assembly, see Paul Achtemeier, "An Elusive Unity: Paul, Acts, and the Early Church," *CBQ* (1986), 1–26.

4. On original sin, see E. B. Cranfield, "On Some of the Problems in the Interpretation of Romans 5:12," *SJT* 22 (1969), 324–41; Herbert Haag, *Is Original Sin in Scripture?* (New York: Sheed and Ward, 1969).

5. R. C. Tannehill, "Dying and Rising with Christ," *BZNW* 57 (1967), 1–43.

6. On law in Pauline thought, see F. F. Bruce, "Paul and the Law of Moses," *BJRL* 57 (1974–75), 259–79; A. Hubner, *Law in Paul's Thought* (Edinburgh: T. and T. Clark, 1984); Joseph Fitzmyer, "Pauline Thought," *The New Jerome Biblical Commentary* (New Jersey: Prentice Hall, 1990), 1402–7.

7. For the emergence of covenant legalism in Old Testament times, see Hillers, *Covenant*, chap. 8.

Chapter 5

1. Nicholas E. Wright, *The Climax of the Covenant* (Minneapolis: Fortress Press, 1992), 231–52.

2. M. J. Suggs, "The Word Is Near You: Romans 10:6–10, Within the Purpose of the Letter," *Christian History and Interpretation* (Cambridge: Cambridge University Press, 1967).

3. For the complete text, see Flannery, *Vatican Council II*, 738–48. For commentary, see Walter Abbott, *The Documents of Vatican II* (New York: America Press, 1966), 656–59.

4. Augustin Bea, *The Church and the Jewish People* (New York: Harper & Row, 1966); Philip Scharper, *Torah and Gospel* (New York: Sheed and Ward, 1966); H. Küng and W. Kasper, eds., *Christians and Jews* (New York: Seabury Press, 1974); Arthur Eckardt, *Your People, My People* (New York: Quadrangle, 1974); George Knight, ed., *Jews and Christianity* (Philadelphia: Westminster Press, 1965).

Chapter 6

1. W. Baird, "Letters of Recommendation: A Study of 2 Cor 3:1–3," *JBL* 80 (1961), 166–72.

2. S. Westerholm, "Letter and Spirit: The Foundation of Pauline Ethics," *NTS* 20 (1984), 229–48.

3. Noteworthy studies on Hebrews include Frederick Bruce, *The Epistle to the Hebrews* (Grand Rapids: Eerdmans, 1990); Ceslaus Spicq, *L'Epitre aux Hebreux* (Paris: J. Gabalda, 1952–53); P. Ellingworth, *The Epistle to the Hebrews* (Grand Rapids: Eerdmans, 1992); Myles Bourke, "The Epistle to the Hebrews," *NJBC* (New Jersey: Prentice Hall, 1990).

4. Colin Brown, ed., *New International Dictionary of New Testament Theology*, "Love" (vol. 2) (Grand Rapids: Zondervan, 1975–85), 538–47.

5. On theology as an academic discipline and as an expression of faith, see Andrew Louth, *Discerning the Mystery* (Oxford: Clarendon, 1983).

6. Ibid.

7. Albert Gelin, *The Poor of Yahweh* (Collegeville: Liturgical Press, 1963).

8. Ibid.

Chapter 7

1. Karl Rahner, *Faith in a Wintry Season* (New York: Crossroad, 1990), 146–47.

2. Carl Braaten, ed., "Justification," *Christian Dogmatics* (vol. 2) (Philadelphia: Fortress Press, 1984), 399–469; Werner Elert, *Law and Gospel* (Philadelphia: Fortress Press, 1967).

3. Flannery, *Vatican Council II*, "Mysterium Ecclesiae" (vol. 2), 428–40.

4. Bernard Häring, *Toward a Christian Moral Theology* (Notre Dame, Ind.: University of Notre Dame Press, 1966).

5. Joachim Jeremias, *The Central Message of the New Testament* (New York: Scribner, 1965); Oscar Cullmann, *The Christology of the New Testament* (Philadelphia: Westminster Press, 1963), 238–45.

6. Flannery, *Vatican Council II*, "Paenitemini" (vol. 2), 1–16.

Chapter 8

1. M. Owen Lee, *First Intermissions* (New York: Oxford University Press, 1995), 130–37.

2. Freedman, *The Anchor Bible Dictionary*, "Holiness" (vol. 3), 237–54.

3. Karl Barth, *The Doctrine of Reconciliation* (Edinburgh: T. and T. Clark, 1956–58); F. W. Dillstone, *The Christian Understanding of Atonement* (London: SCM Press, 1984).

4. Oscar Cullmann, *Baptism in the New Testament* (London: SCM Press, 1950).

5. Freedman, *The Anchor Bible Dictionary*, "Conversion" (vol. 1), 1131–33.

6. On liturgy and community, see Edward Kilmartin, *Christian Liturgy* (Kansas City: Sheed and Ward, 1988); Evelyn Underhill, *Worship* (New York: Crossroad, 1983); J. Tillard, *The Eucharist: Pasch of God's People* (New York: Alba House, 1977).

7. On eucharist and social action, see Frank Henderson, *Liturgy, Justice, and the Reign of God* (New York: Paulist Press, 1989); James Empereur, *The Liturgy that Does Justice* (Collegeville: Liturgical Press, 1990); Monika Hellwig, *The Eucharist and the Hunger of the World* (Kansas City: Sheed and Ward, 1992).

Scripture Index

OLD TESTAMENT